$500,000* Worth of
Inspiring Quotations
For Our Times

action **attitude** change character children
enemies **failure** family friends goals government happiness
humor initiative knowledge **leadership**
learning **life** love optimism parenting pessimism politics
relationships **success** time wisdom

* Far more practical wisdom and wit regarding life, love, attitude, happiness, leadership, success, character and more than you would gain from earning BA, MA and PhD degrees!

Compiled by

Web Augustine

ISBN 978-0-578-08510-4

Please visit Zinfandel Publishing (www.zinfandelpublishing.com) for more information about this book.

Note from the Compiler

I would like to dedicate this book of quotations to my loving wife, Carol, who is always supportive of me taking on interesting, but time consuming projects like this. May the wisdom and insight collected here benefit my wonderful children, Lauren and Michael, and my stepdaughters, Ashley and Kristin Ferrell, as they continue their own journeys through college, early careers and the rest of what I am sure will be very interesting lives!

This list of my favorite 1,400 quotations was collected over many years and self-published via LuLu Enterprises Inc. (www.lulu.com) in June 2011.

I would like to thank Wikipedia (www.wikipedia.org) for many of the brief biographies of quotation authors included with the quotations whenever possible.

Enjoy!

Web

Web Augustine
Menlo Park, CA

Quotations by Primary Tag (1,401)

Selected Quotations by Author

Table of Contents

Favorite Quotations

Indices

action accomplishment beginning castles change decision delay domination dream effort formulation goals hard work harvest implementation inactivity initiative intelligence intent job perseverance plan priority proactive procrastination seeds sitting stumble talent timing wish work

"A dream is just a dream. A goal is a dream with a plan and a deadline."

Harvey MacKay (1932 -), American businessman, columnist and author.

"A goal without a plan is just a wish."

Antoine de Saint Exupéry (1900 - 1944), French writer and aviator. He is best remembered for his novella "The Little Prince" ("Le Petit Prince").

"A road well begun is the battle half won. The important thing is to make a beginning and get under way."

Sören Kierkegaard (1813 - 1855), Danish philosopher, theologian and author.

"A wish changes nothing. A decision changes everything."

Unknown

"Change the changeable, accept the unchangeable, and remove yourself from the unacceptable."

Denis Waitley (1933 -), American motivational speaker and writer, consultant and best-selling author.

"Continuous effort - not strength or intelligence - is the key to unlocking our potential."

Sir Winston Churchill (1874 - 1965), British orator, author and Prime Minister during World War II.

"Do not wait; the time will never be 'just right.' Start where you stand, and work with whatever tools you may have at your command, and better tools will be found as you go along."

Napoleon Hill (1883 - 1970), American author who was one of the earliest producers of the modern genre of personal-success literature.

"Do or do not, there is no try."

Yoda, Jedi master, from the "Star Wars" movie series.

"Don't be a time manager, be a priority manager. Cut your major goals into bite-sized pieces. Each small priority or requirement on the way to ultimate goal becomes a mini goal in itself."

Denis Waitley (1933 -), American motivational speaker and writer, consultant and best-selling author.

"Don't be afraid to give your best to what seemingly are small jobs. Every time you conquer one it makes you that much stronger. If you do the little jobs well, the big ones will tend to take care of themselves."

Dale Carnegie (1888 - 1955), American writer, lecturer, and the developer of famous courses in self-improvement, salesmanship, corporate training, public speaking, and interpersonal skills. He's best known as author of "How to Win Friends and Influence People" (1936).

"Don't judge each day by the harvest you reap, but by the seeds you plant."

Robert Louis Stevenson (1850 - 1894), Scottish writer.

"Even if you are on the right track, you'll get run over if you just sit there."

Will Rogers (1879 -1935) Cherokee-American cowboy, social commentator.

"Far and away the best prize that life offers is the chance to work hard at work worth doing."

Theodore Roosevelt (1858 - 1919), 26th US President (1901 - 1909), from a speech in New York, September 7, 1903.

"For an athlete to function properly, he must be intent. There has to be a definite purpose and goal if you are to progress. If you are not intent about what you are doing, you aren't able to resist the temptation to do something else that might be more fun at the moment."

John Wooden (1910 - 2010), American Hall of Fame basketball coach for UCLA who won a record 10 NCAA men's championships.

"Goals provide the energy source that powers our lives. One of the best ways we can get the most from the energy we have is to focus it. That is what goals can do for us; concentrate our energy."

Denis Waitley (1933 -), American motivational speaker and writer, consultant and best-selling author.

"Goals. There's no telling what you can do when you get inspired by them. There's no telling what you can do when you believe in them. There's no telling what will happen when you act upon them."

Jim Rohn (1930 - 2009), American entrepreneur, author and motivational speaker. His rags to riches story played a large part in his work, which influenced others in the personal development industry.

"Hard work spotlights the character of people; some turn up their sleeves, some turn up their noses, and some don't turn up at all!"

Sam Ewing (1949 -), American and former major league baseball player.

"I have been impressed with the urgency of doing. Knowing is not enough; we must apply. Being willing is not enough; we must do."

Leonardo da Vinci (1452 - 1519), Italian architect, engineer, painter, sculptor, inventor and scientist.

"If not you, who? If not now, when?"

Vince Lombardi (1913 - 1970), American football coach best known as the head coach of the Green Bay Packers during the 1960s.

"If you don't do it, you'll never know what would have happened if you had done it."

Ashleigh Brilliant (1933 -), British-born American author and syndicated cartoonist.

"If you fail to prepare, you prepare to fail."

John Wooden (1910 - 2010), American Hall of Fame basketball coach for UCLA who won a record 10 NCAA men's championships.

"If you follow in others footsteps you will never leave yours behind."

Unknown

"If you have built castles in the air, your work need not be lost. There is where they should be. Now put foundations under them."

Henry David Thoreau (1817 - 1862), American writer, poet and philosopher.

"If you want to know your past - look into your present conditions. If you want to know your future - look into your present actions."

Buddhist saying.

"If you want to reach a goal, you must 'see the reaching' in your own mind before you actually arrive at your goal."

Zig Ziglar (1926 -), American author, salesman, and motivational speaker.

"Implementation is always harder than formulation. 90% know what needs to be done to be successful. Only 5% do it."

Unknown

"It had long since come to my attention that people of accomplishment rarely sat back and let things happen to them. They went out and happened to things."

Leonardo da Vinci (1452 - 1519), Italian architect, engineer, painter, sculptor, inventor and scientist.

"It is not enough to have a good mind. The main thing is to use it well."

Rene Descartes (1596 - 1650), a natural philosopher and writer who spent most of his adult life in the Dutch Republic. He has been dubbed the "Father of Modern Philosophy", and much subsequent Western philosophy is a response to his writings, which are studied closely to this day.

"It is not only what we do, but also what we do not do, for which we are accountable."

Moliere (1622 – 1673), French actor, playwright and one of the greatest of all writers of French comedy.

"Keep on going, and the chances are that you will stumble on something, perhaps when you are least expecting it. I never heard of anyone stumbling on something sitting down."

Charles F. Kettering (1876 - 1958), American inventor, engineer, businessman, and the holder of 140 patents.

"Motivation is what gets you started. Habit is what keeps you going."

Jim Rohn (1930 - 2009), American entrepreneur, author and motivational speaker. His rags to riches story played a large part in his work, which influenced others in the personal development industry.

"My grandfather once told me that there were two kinds of people: those who do the work and those who take the credit. He told me to try to be in the first group; there was much less competition."

Indira Gandhi (1917 - 1984), the third Prime Minister of the Republic of India for three consecutive terms from 1966 to 1977 and for a fourth term from 1980 until her assassination in 1984.

"People may not always believe what you say, but they will believe what you do."

Unknown

"Put yourself in a state of mind where you can say to yourself, 'Here is an opportunity for you to celebrate like never before, my own power, my own ability to get myself to do whatever is necessary.'"

Anthony Robbins (1960 -), American self-help author and success coach. His books include "Unlimited Power: The New Science of Personal Achievement" and "Awaken The Giant Within."

"Some people dream of success while others wake up and work hard at it."

Unknown

"Some people want it to happen, some wish it would happen, others make it happen."

Michael Jordan (1963 -), former American professional basketball player, active businessman, and majority owner of the Charlotte Bobcats. Considered the greatest basketball player of all time.

"Take time to deliberate; but when the time for action arrives, stop thinking and go in."

Napoleon Bonaparte (1769 - 1821), French military and political leader during the latter stages of the French Revolution.

"The more you are willing to accept responsibility for your actions, the more credibility you will have."

Brian Koslow, American author and entrepreneur.

"The only thing that separates the successful people from the ones who aren't is the willingness to work very, very hard."

Helen Gurley Brown (1922 -), American writer and editor of *Cosmopolitan* magazine.

"The reason why people do not obtain success is because it is disguised as hard work."

Unknown

"The secret of getting ahead is getting started. The secret of getting started is breaking your complex overwhelming tasks into small manageable tasks, and then starting on the first one."

Mark Twain, the pen name of Samuel Langhorne Clemens (1835 - 1910), American writer and humorist.

"The tragedy of life doesn't lie in not reaching your goal. The tragedy lies in having no goal to reach."

Benjamin Mays (1894 - 1984), American minister, educator, scholar, social activist, and the president of Morehouse College in Atlanta, Georgia, from 1940 to 1967. He was also a significant mentor to civil rights leader Martin Luther King Jr.

"The ultimate reason for setting goals is to entice you to become the person it takes to achieve them."

Jim Rohn (1930 - 2009), American entrepreneur, author and motivational speaker. His rags to riches story played a large part in his work, which influenced others in the personal development industry.

"The world does not need tourists who ride by in a bus clucking their tongues. The world as it is needs those who will love it enough to change it, with what they have, where they are."

Robert Fulghum (1937 -), American author, painter, sculptor and former minister.

"There are three types of people in this world: those who make things happen, those who watch things happen and those who wonder what happened."

Unknown

"There are three ways to obtain wealth: inheritance, luck, and hard work. None is guaranteed, but you have no influence over the first two."

Unknown

"Though no one can go back and make a brand new start, anyone can start from now and make a brand new ending."

Carl Bard

"To map out a course of action and follow it to an end requires courage."

Ralph Waldo Emerson (1803 - 1882), American writer and poet.

"We only grow when we step outside our comfort zone."

Unknown

"What you do, or dream you can, begin it. Boldness has genius, power and magic in it. Begin it now."

Johann Wolfgang von Goethe (1749 - 1832), German writer, philosopher and scientist.

"When you can do the common things of life in an uncommon way, you will command the attention of the world."

George Washington Carver (1864 - 1943), American scientist, botanist, educator, and inventor. Much of Carver's fame is based on his research into and promotion of crops as alternatives to cotton, such as peanuts and sweet potatoes.

"You must take action now that will move you towards your goals. Develop a sense of urgency in your life."

H. Jackson Brown, Jr., American best selling writer and author of "Life's Little Instruction Book."

accomplishments anger **attitude** behavior belief

confidence conversation convince courage criticism dreams

enthusiasm excellence fear foregiveness forgiveness future genius goal

habit ideas ignorance impossible insanity lies life listen mediocre mind

mistakes passion past people perseverance persistence personal

personal growth perspective preparation progress risk smile

stupidity talk truth understand value vision words work

"A great attitude does much more than turn on the lights in our worlds; it seems to magically connect us to all sorts of serendipitous opportunities that were somehow absent before the change."

Earl Nightingale (1921 - 1989), American motivational speaker and author, known as the "Dean of Personal Development."

"A great life is not about routine but doing something rare. To cherish and not compare. To forgive, not to blame and to be loving without counting. Laugh at your mistakes but learn from them. Joke over your troubles but gather strength from them. Have fun with your difficulties but overcome them."

Unknown

"A great many people think they are thinking when they are merely rearranging their prejudices."

William James (1842 - 1910), a pioneering American psychologist and philosopher who was trained as a medical doctor. He wrote influential books on the young science of psychology, educational psychology, psychology of religious experience and mysticism, and on the philosophy of pragmatism.

"A happy heart is good medicine and a positive mind works healing. In your busy schedule, don't forget to smile and have a good laugh because it adds color to your life."

Unknown

"A lie has speed, but truth has endurance."

Edgar J. Mohn

"A little lie is like a little pregnancy: it doesn't take long before everyone knows."

C.S. Lewis (1898 - 1963), Irish-born British novelist, academic, medievalist, literary critic, essayist, and lay theologian. He is well known for his fictional work, especially "The Screwtape Letters" and "The Chronicles of Narnia."

"A long dispute means that both parties are wrong."

Voltaire (1694 - 1778), French writer and philosopher.

"A man convinced against his will is still of the same opinion."

Unknown

"A man is about as big as the things that make him angry."

Sir Winston Churchill (1874 - 1965), British orator, author and Prime Minister during World War II.

"A man is not finished when he is defeated, he is finished when he quits."

Richard Nixon (1913 - 1994), 37th US President.

"A man spends the first half of his life learning habits that shorten the other half of his life."

Unknown

"A man who has never lost himself in a cause bigger than himself has missed one of life's mountaintop experiences. Only in losing himself does he find himself. Only then does he discover all the latent strengths he never knew he had and which otherwise would have remained dormant."

Richard Nixon (1913 - 1994), 37th US President.

"A mind once stretched by a new idea never regains its original dimension."

Oliver Wendell Holmes (1809 - 1894), American physician, poet, writer, humorist and Professor at Harvard.

"A person who can speak many languages is not necessarily more valuable than a person who can listen in one."

Unknown

"A player who makes a team great is much more valuable than a great player."

John Wooden (1910 - 2010), American Hall of Fame basketball coach for UCLA. Won a record 10 NCAA men's championships.

"A smart man covers his ass, a wise man leaves his pants on."

C.D. Bailey

"A tear shed can say more than a hundred words spoken."

Unknown

"Ability is what you're capable of doing. Motivation determines what you do. Attitude determines how well you do it."

Raymond Chandler (1888 - 1959), Anglo-American novelist and screenwriter who had an immense stylistic influence upon the modern private detective story, especially in the style of the writing and the attitudes now characteristic of the genre. His protagonist, Philip Marlowe, along with Dashiell Hammett's Sam Spade, is considered synonymous with "private detective", both being played on screen by Humphrey Bogart.

"Ability will never catch up with the demand for it."

Malcolm S. Forbes (1919 - 1919), American publisher of Forbes magazine.

"Admit to a lie and it will always be in your past; if you don't it will always be in your future."

Unknown

"Adversity has the effect of eliciting talents, which in prosperous circumstances would have lain dormant."

Horace (65 BC - 8BC), the leading Roman lyric poet during the time of Augustus.

"All my life, I always wanted to be somebody. Now I see that I should have been more specific."

Jane Wagner (1935 -), American writer, director and producer. Wagner is best known as Lily Tomlin's comedy writer, collaborator and life partner.

"All of us do not have equal talent, but all of us should have an equal opportunity to develop our talent."

John F. Kennedy (1917 - 1963), 35th US President (1961 - 1963).

"Always do right. This will gratify some people and astonish the rest."

Mark Twain, the pen name of Samuel Langhorne Clemens (1835 – 1910), American writer and humorist.

"Always remember you're unique, just like everyone else."

Alison Boulter

"An angry person is seldom reasonable; a reasonable person is seldom angry."

Unknown

"An atheist is a man who has no invisible means of support."

John Buchan (1875 - 1940), Scottish author and politician.

"An error doesn't become a mistake until you choose to ignore it."

Unknown

"Anger is costly on the soul, be careful with what you choose to spend it on."

Bohdan Chreptak

"Anger is the most impotent of passions. It effects nothing it goes about, and hurts the one who is possessed by it more than the one against whom it is directed."

Carl Sandburg (1878 - 1967), American historian, poet and novelist.

"Anger opens the mouth and shuts the mind."

Unknown

"Anger, if not restrained, is frequently more hurtful to us than the injury that provokes it."

Seneca (~ 54 BC - ~ 39 AD), Roman rhetorician and writer.

"Anyone can become angry - that is easy, but to be angry with the right person, to the right degree, at the right time, for the right purpose and in the right way - that is not easy."

Aristotle (384 - 322 BC), Greek writer, teacher and philosopher, often considered the father of logic.

"As I get older, I've learned to listen to people rather than accuse them of things."

Po Bronson (1964 -), American journalist and author. Quoted in *Publishers Weekly*.

"As I grow older, I pay less attention to what men say. I just watch what they do."

Andrew Carnegie, (1835-1919), Scottish-born American industrialist and philanthropist.

"As long as you put in the work, you can own the dream. When the work stops, the dream disappears."

Jim Dietz

"Attitude is a little thing that makes a big difference."

Sir Winston Churchill (1874 - 1965), British orator, author and Prime Minister during World War II.

"Attitude is more important than the past, than education, than money, than circumstances, than what people do or say. It is more important than appearance, giftedness, or skill."

W.C. Fields (1880 - 1946), American comedian, actor, juggler and writer. Fields was known for his comic persona as a misanthropic and hard-drinking egotist who remained a sympathetic character despite his snarling contempt for dogs, children, and women.

"Be nice to people on your way up because you meet them on your way down."

Jimmy Durante (1893 - 1980), American comedian, pianist and singer.

"Be not afraid of growing slowly, be afraid only of standing still."

Chinese proverb.

"Be profound, be funny, or be quiet!!"

Albert Einstein (1879 - 1955), German-born American physicist who developed the theories of relativity and won the Nobel Prize for Physics in 1921.

"Be real. Try to do what you say, say what you mean, and be what you seem."

Marian Wright Edelman (1939 -) American activist and founder of the Children's Defense Fund.

"Be true to your work, your word and your friend."

Henry David Thoreau (1817 - 1862), American writer, poet and philosopher.

"Be who you are and say what you feel because those who mind don't matter and those who matter don't mind."

Dr. Seuss (1904 - 1991), the penname of Theodor Geisel, American writer and cartoonist most widely known for his children's books.

"Before you can win, you have to believe you are worthy."

Mike Ditka (1939 -), former American football NFL player, television commentator, and coach. Ditka coached the Chicago Bears for 11 years and New Orleans Saints for three years.

"Begin each day as if it were on purpose."

Mary Anne Radmacher

"Believe in yourself. You gain strength, courage, and confidence by every experience in which you stop to look fear in the face. . . You must do that which you think you cannot do."

Eleanor Roosevelt (1884 - 1962), 32nd US first lady (1933 - 1945), UN diplomat, humanitarian.

"Better to remain silent and be thought a fool than to speak out and remove all doubt."

Abraham Lincoln (1809 - 1865), 16th US President. His term of office was from 1861 to 1865 and included the American Civil War.

"Champions aren't made in the gyms. Champions are made from something they have deep inside them -- a desire, a dream, a vision."

Muhammad Ali (1942 -), former American boxer and three-time World Heavyweight Champion, who is widely considered one of the greatest heavyweight championship boxers.

"Common sense is a most uncommon virtue."

Mark Twain, the pen name of Samuel Langhorne Clemens (1835 – 1910), American writer and humorist.

"Common sense is not so common."

Voltaire (1694 - 1778), French writer and philosopher.

"Common sense is the collection of prejudices acquired by age eighteen."

Albert Einstein (1879 - 1955), German-born American physicist who developed the theories of relativity who won the Nobel Prize for Physics in 1921.

"Courage doesn't not always roar. Sometimes courage is the small voice at the end of the day that says, 'I will try again tomorrow.'"

Mary Anne Radmacher

"Courage is being afraid but going on anyhow."

Dan Rather (1931 -), American journalist and the former news anchor for the CBS Evening News.

"Courage is fear holding on a minute longer."

General George S. Patton Jr. (1885 - 1945), American Army officer best known for his leadership while commanding corps and armies as a general during World War II. He was also well known for his eccentricity and controversial outspokenness.

"Courage is not the absence of fear, but rather the judgment that something else is more important than fear. Courage is the presence of fear with the capacity to manage and overcome it."

Ambrose Redmoon, pseudonym for James Neil Hollingworth (1933–1996), a beatnik, hippie, writer, and former manager of the psychedelic folk rock band Quicksilver Messenger Service.

"Courage is resistance to fear, mastery of fear - not absence of fear."

Mark Twain, the pen name of Samuel Langhorne Clemens (1835 – 1910), American writer and humorist.

"Courage is what it takes to stand up and speak. Courage is also what it takes to sit down and listen."

Sir Winston Churchill (1874 - 1965), British orator, author and Prime Minister during World War II.

"Criticism should always leave people with the feeling that they have been helped."

Unknown

"Cynicism is an unpleasant way of saying the truth."

Lillian Hellman (1905 - 1984), American playwright, linked throughout her life with many left-wing causes. From "The Little Foxes" (1939).

"Determination gives you the resolve to keep going in spite of the roadblocks that lay before you."

Denis Waitley (1933 -), American motivational speaker and writer, consultant and best-selling author.

"Discipline is the bridge between goals and accomplishments."

Jim Rohn (1930 - 2009), American entrepreneur, author and motivational speaker. His rags to riches story played a large part in his work, which influenced others in the personal development industry.

"Discover the tools to build your own vision."

Mary Anne Radmacher

"Do not lose hold of your dreams or aspirations. For if you do, you may still exist but you have ceased to live."

Henry David Thoreau (1817 - 1862), American writer, poet and philosopher.

"Do not unto others that you would not have them do unto you."

The Silver Rule (a negative / prohibitive form of the Golden Rule).

"Don't ask what the world needs. Ask what makes you come alive, and go do it. Because what the world needs is people who have come alive."

Howard Thurman (1899 - 1981), influential American author, philosopher, theologian, educator and civil rights leader.

"Don't dwell on the past ... learn from it."

Denis Waitley (1933 -), American motivational speaker and writer, consultant and best-selling author.

"Don't find fault, find a remedy."

Henry Ford (1863 - 1947), prominent American industrialist, the founder of the Ford Motor Company, and sponsor of the development of the assembly line technique of mass production.

"Don't let a negative experience of your past be the defining moment of your future."

Unknown

"Don't let someone else's opinion of you become your reality."

Les Brown

"Don't let what you cannot do interfere with what you can do."

John Wooden (1910 - 2010), American Hall of Fame basketball coach for UCLA who won a record 10 NCAA men's championships.

"Don't let yesterday take up too much of today."

Will Rogers (1879 -1935) Cherokee-American cowboy, social commentator.

"Don't wait for, expect, or rely on favors. Count on earning them by hard work and perseverance."

Marian Wright Edelman (1939 -), American activist and Founder of the Children's Defense Fund.

"Don't waste your time on jealousy. Sometimes you're ahead, sometimes you're behind. The race is long and, in the end, it's only with yourself."

Baz Luhrmann (1962 -), Australian film director, screenwriter, and producer best known for The Red Curtain Trilogy, which includes his films *Strictly Ballroom*, *William Shakespeare's Romeo + Juliet* and *Moulin Rouge!*. In 2008, he released his film *Australia*, starring Hugh Jackman and Nicole Kidman.

"Dream is not what you see in sleep; dream is something that doesn't let you sleep."

Dr. A.P.J Abdul Kalam, Indian aeronautical engineer, Professor and the 11th President of India (2002 - 2007).

"Empty pockets never held anyone back. Only empty heads and empty hearts can do that."

Norman Vincent Peale (1898 - 1993), American minister and author (most notably of *The Power of Positive Thinking*) and a progenitor of the theory of "positive thinking".

"Every defeat, every heartbreak, every loss, contains its own seed, its own lesson on how to improve your performance the next time."

Og Mandino (1923 - 1996), American author who wrote the bestselling book "The Greatest Salesman in the World."

"Every job is a self-portrait of the person who did it. Autograph your work with excellence."

Jessica Guidobono

"Everyone likes a compliment."

Abraham Lincoln (1809 - 1865), 16th US President. His term of office was from 1861 to 1865 and included the American Civil War.

"Everywhere you go, take a smile with you."

Sasha Azevedo, American actress, athlete and model.

"Excellence is an art won by training and habituation. We do not act rightly because we have virtue or excellence, but rather we have those because we have acted rightly. We are what we repeatedly do. Excellence, then, is not an act but a habit."

Aristotle (384 - 322 BC), Greek writer, teacher and philosopher, often considered the father of logic.

"Excellence is the result of caring more than others think is wise, risking more than others think is safe, dreaming more than others think is practical, and expecting more than others think is possible."

Unknown

"Exhilaration is that feeling you get just after a great idea hits you, and just before you realize what's wrong with it."

Joe Moore

"Expect the best, plan for the worst, and prepare to be surprised."

Denis Waitley (1933 -), American motivational speaker and writer, consultant and best-selling author.

"Facts do not cease to exist because they are ignored."

Aldous Huxley (1894 - 1963), English writer and author of "Brave New World."

"Fall down seven times, get up eight."

Japanese proverb.

"First seek to understand, then seek to be understood."

Stephen R. Covey (1932 -), Professor and author best known for the best-selling book, "The Seven Habits of Highly Effective People."

"For good or ill, your conversation is your advertisement. Every time you open your mouth you let the people look into your mind."

Bruce Barton (1886 - 1967), American advertising executive and US congressman.

"Forgiveness is almost a selfish act because of its immense benefits to the one who forgives."

Lawana Blackwell

"Forgiveness does not change the past, but it does enlarge the future."

Paul Boese

"Forgiveness is abandoning all hope of changing the past."

Lily Tomlin (1939 -), American actress and comedian.

"Genius is 1% inspiration and 99% perspiration."

Thomas Edison (1847 - 1931), American inventor and salesman who frequently worked more than 40 hours straight.

"Genius is the ability to put into effect what is on your mind."

F. Scott Fitzgerald (1896 - 1940), American novelist.

"God wisely designed the human body so we can neither pat our own backs nor kick ourselves too easily."

Unknown

"Good is the enemy of GREAT!"

Jim Collins (1958 -), American business consultant, author, and lecturer on the subject of company sustainability and growth.

"Good, better, best. Never let it rest until your good is better then best!"

Unknown

"Great effort springs naturally from great attitude."

Pat Riley (1945 -), former American professional basketball player and then head coach in the NBA. Currently, he is team President of the Miami Heat. Widely regarded as one of the greatest NBA coaches of all time, Riley has served as the head coach of five championship teams.

"Great minds discuss ideas; average minds discuss events; small minds discuss people."

Eleanor Roosevelt (1884 - 1962), 32nd US first lady (1933 - 1945), UN diplomat, humanitarian.

"Great minds have purposes, others have wishes."

Washington Irving (1783 - 1859), American writer and historian.

"Great spirits have always encountered violent opposition from mediocre minds."

Albert Einstein (1879 - 1955), German-born American physicist who developed the theories of relativity and won the Nobel Prize for Physics in 1921.

"Great things are not done by impulse, but by a series of small things brought together."

Vincent van Gogh (1853 - 1890), Dutch painter.

"Having a positive mental attitude is asking how something can be done rather than saying it can't be done."

Bo Bennett

"He has the right to criticize who has the heart to help."

Abraham Lincoln (1809 - 1865), 16th US President. His term of office was from 1861 to 1865 and included the American Civil War.

"He who angers you controls you!"

Elizabeth Kenny (1880 - 1952), Australian pioneering physical therapist.

"He who builds to every man's advice will have a crooked house."

Danish proverb.

"He who does not know how to look back at where he came from will never get to his destination."

Jose Rizal (1861 - 1896), a Filipino polymath, patriot and the most prominent advocate for reforms in the Philippines during the Spanish colonial era.

"He who laughs, lasts."

Robert Fulghum (1937 -), American author, painter, sculptor and former minister.

"Help identify the shallow end of the gene pool - Do Drugs."

Unknown

"Here's to the crazy ones. The misfits. The rebels. The trouble-makers. The round pegs in the square holes. The ones who see things differently. They're not fond of rules, and they have no respect for the status-quo. You can quote them, disagree with them, glorify, or vilify them. But the only thing you can't do is ignore them. Because they change things. They push the human race forward. And while some may see them as the crazy ones, we see genius. Because the people who are crazy enough to think they can change the world, are the ones who do."

Steve Jobs (1955 -), American businessman and Co-Founder at Apple Inc., the inventor of Mac computers, iPods, iPhones and iPads.

"High performers carefully rethink their strategy at each hilltop."

Unknown

"Hold fast your dreams! Within your heart keep one still, secret spot where dreams may go and, sheltered so, may thrive and grow."

Louise Driscoll

"Holding onto anger is like grasping onto a hot coal with the intent of throwing it at someone else. You are the one who gets burned."

Gautama Buddha, a spiritual teacher who founded Buddhism.

"How wonderful it is that nobody need wait a single moment before starting to improve the world."

Anne Frank (1929 - 1945), one of the most renowned and most discussed Jewish victims of the Holocaust. Acknowledged for the quality of her writing, her diary has become one of the world's most widely read books, and has been the basis for several plays and films.

"Human beings, by changing the inner attitudes of their minds, can change the outer aspects of their lives."

William James (1842 - 1910), a pioneering American psychologist and philosopher who was trained as a medical doctor. He wrote influential books on the young science of psychology, educational psychology, psychology of religious experience and mysticism, and on the philosophy of pragmatism.

"I am the master of my unspoken words, and a slave to those that should have remained unspoken."

Unknown

"I am the world's greatest authority on my own opinion."

Unknown

"I believe that the level of success we experience in life is in direct proportion to the level of our commitment to CANI!, to Constant and Never-Ending Improvement."

Anthony Robbins (1960 -), American self-help author and success coach. His books include "Unlimited Power: The New Science of Personal Achievement" and "Awaken the Giant Within."

"I can explain it to you, but I can't understand it for you."

Unknown

"I certainly don't regret my experiences because without them, I couldn't imagine who or where I would be today. Life is an amazing gift to those who have overcome great obstacles, and attitude is everything!"

Sasha Azevedo, American actress, athlete and model.

"I cried because I had no shoes and then I saw the man with no feet."

Unknown

"I discovered I always have choices and sometimes it's only a choice of attitude."

Judith M. Knowlton

"I do not say that all men are equal in their ability, character and motivation. I do say that every American should be given a fair chance to develop all the talents they may have."

John F. Kennedy (1917 - 1963), 35th US President (1961 - 1963).

"I don't have an attitude problem. You have a perception problem."

Roz Triebner

"I don't need your attitude; I have one of my own."

Unknown

"I have never been a material girl. My father always told me never to love anything that cannot love you back."

Imelda Marcos (1929 -), Filipino politician and wife of 10th Philippine President Ferdinand Marcos. Upon the ascension of her husband to political power, she held various positions in the government until 1986.

"I have opinions of my own -- strong opinions -- but I don't always agree with them."

George H.W. Bush (1924 -), 41st US President (1989 - 1993).

"I hear and I forget. I see and I remember. I do and I understand."

Confucius (551 BC - 479 BC), Chinese writer and philosopher.

"I know I'm drinking myself to a slow death, but then I'm in no hurry."

Robert Benchley (1889 - 1945), American humorist best known for his work as a newspaper columnist and film actor.

"I live in the present. I only remember the past, and anticipate the future."

Henry David Thoreau (1817 - 1862), American writer, poet and philosopher.

"I prefer the errors of enthusiasm to the indifference of wisdom."

Anatole France (1844 - 1924), French poet, journalist, and novelist.

"I saw the angel in the marble and carved until I set him free."

Michelangelo (1475 - 1564), Italian sculptor, painter, poet and architect of the Renaissance.

"I think that somehow, we learn who we really are and then live with that decision."

Eleanor Roosevelt (1884 - 1962), 32nd US first lady (1933 - 1945), UN diplomat, humanitarian.

"I would rather have a mind opened by wonder than one closed by belief."

Gerry Spence (1929 -), American trial lawyer.

"Idealism increases in direct proportion to one's distance from the problem."

John Galsworthy (1867 - 1933), English novelist and playwright who won the Nobel Prize in Literature (1932).

"If all you have is a hammer, everything looks like a nail."

Abraham Maslow in "The Psychology of Science", published in 1966.

"If everything seems to be going well, you have obviously overlooked something."

Unknown

"If I had eight hours to chop down a tree, I'd spend six hours sharpening my ax."

Abraham Lincoln (1809 - 1865), 16th US President. His term of office was from 1861 to 1865 and included the American Civil War.

"If I were two-faced, would I be wearing this one?"

Abraham Lincoln (1809 - 1865), 16th US President. His term of office was from 1861 to 1865 and included the American Civil War.

"If it takes a lot of words to say what you have in mind, give it more thought."

Dennis Roch

"If we all do one random act of kindness daily, we just might set the world in the right direction."

Martin Kornfeld

"If we couldn't laugh, we would all go insane."

Jimmy Buffet (1946 -), American singer, songwriter, author, businessman, and movie producer. He is best known for his music, which often portrays an "island escapism" lifestyle.

"If you are going to achieve excellence in big things, you develop the habit in little matters. Excellence is not an exception, it is a prevailing attitude."

Colin Powell (1937 -), former General and US Secretary of State (2001 – 2005).

"If you are going to walk on thin ice you might as well dance."

Unknown

"If you are patient in one moment of anger, you will escape a hundred days of sorrow."

Chinese proverb.

"If you believe you can, you probably can. If you believe you won't, you most assuredly won't. Belief is the ignition switch that gets you off the launching pad."

Denis Waitley (1933 -), American motivational speaker and writer, consultant and best-selling author.

"If you can't solve a problem, it's because you're playing by the rules."

Paul Arden (1940 - 2008), influential author of several books on advertising and motivation including "Whatever You Think, Think The Opposite" and "It's Not How Good You Are, It's How Good You Want To Be" and a former creative director for Saatchi and Saatchi at the height of their advertising might.

"If you can't convince them, confuse them."

Harry S. Truman (1884 – 1972), 33rd US President (1945 - 1953).

"If you can't run with the big dogs, then stay on the porch with the puppies!"

Unknown

"If you do not respect yourself, do not expect others to do so."

Unknown

"If you don't have time to do it right, when will you have time to do it over?"

John Wooden (1910 - 2010), American Hall of Fame basketball coach for UCLA who won a record 10 NCAA men's championships.

"If you don't know where you're going how do you expect to get there?"

Unknown

"If you love what you do, you will never work another day in your life."

Confucius (551 BC - 479 BC), Chinese writer and philosopher.

"If you stand up to be counted, from time to time you may get yourself knocked down. But remember this: a man flattened by an opponent can get up again. A man flattened by conformity stays down for good."

Thomas J. Watson, Jr. (1914 - 1993), American businessman and President of IBM (1952 - 1971).

"If you wait to do everything until you're sure it's right, you'll probably never do much of anything."

Win Borden

"If you're enthusiastic about the things you're working on, people will come ask you to do interesting things."

James Woolsey (1941 -), American foreign policy specialist and former head of the Central Intelligence Agency.

"If you're trying to achieve, there will be roadblocks. I've had them; everybody has had them. But obstacles don't have to stop you. If you run into a wall, don't turn around and give up. Figure out how to climb it, go through it, or work around it."

Michael Jordan (1963 -), former American professional basketball player, active businessman, and majority owner of the Charlotte Bobcats. Considered the greatest basketball player of all time.

"I'm not young enough to know everything."

James Matthew Barries (1860 - 1937), Scottish dramatist and novelist best known as the creator of Peter Pan.

"Imagination is the eye of the soul."

Joseph Joubert (1754 -1824), French essayist and moralist.

"In matters of principle, stand like a rock."

Thomas Jefferson (1743 - 1826), 3rd US President (1801 - 1809) and the primary writer of the Declaration of Independence in 1776.

"In teaching, and almost any other profession, they won't care how much you know until they know how much you care."

Unknown

"In the field of observation, chance favors only the prepared mind."

Louis Pasteur (1822-1895), French chemist and biologist in an 1854 lecture.

"Insanity is doing the same thing over again and expecting different results."

Albert Einstein (1879 - 1955), German-born American physicist who developed the theories of relativity and won the Nobel Prize for Physics in 1921.

"Instead of worrying about what people say of you, why not spend time trying to accomplish something they will admire."

Dale Carnegie (1888 - 1955), American writer, lecturer, and the developer of famous courses in self-improvement, salesmanship, corporate training, public speaking, and interpersonal skills. He's best known as author of "How to Win Friends and Influence People" (1936).

"Integrity is the essence of everything successful."

Richard Buckminster "Bucky" Fuller, (1895 - 1983), American engineer, author, designer, inventor, and futurist. Fuller published more than 30 books, and developed numerous inventions, mainly architectural designs, the best known of which is the geodesic dome. Carbon molecules known as fullerenes were later named by scientists for their resemblance to geodesic spheres.

"It is a miracle curiosity survives formal education."

Albert Einstein (1879 - 1955), German-born American physicist who developed the theories of relativity and won the Nobel Prize for Physics in 1921.

"It is always the ones who talk loudest who do the least."

Unknown

"It is always the right time to do the right thing."

Martin Luther King Jr. (1929 - 1968), American civil rights leader and Nobel Peace Prize winner.

"It is difficult to say what is impossible, for the dream of yesterday is the hope of today and the reality of tomorrow."

Robert H. Goddard (1882 - 1945), American professor, physicist and inventor who is credited with creating and building the world's first liquid-fueled rocket, which he successfully launched on March 16, 1926.

"It is nice to be important, but much more important to be nice."

Unknown

"It is not who is right, but what is right, that is important."

Thomas Henry Huxley (1825 - 1895), English biologist, known as "Darwin's Bulldog" for his advocacy of Charles Darwin's theory of evolution.

"It is part of the unceasing human endeavor to prove that the spirit of man can transcend the flaws of his own nature."

Aung San Suu Kyi (1945 -), Burmese opposition politician and a leading human rights activist.

"It takes 20 years to build a reputation and five minutes to ruin it. If you think about that, you'll do things differently."

Warren Buffett (1930 -), American investor, businessman and philanthropist.

"It takes 72 muscles to frown and only 14 to smile."

Unknown

"It takes less time to do a thing right that it does to explain why you did it wrong."

Henry Wadsworth Longfellow (1807 - 1882), American writer and poet.

"It's never too late to be who you always wanted to be."

George Eliot (1819 - 1880), pen name of English writer Mary Ann Evans.

"It's not enough that we do our best; sometimes we have to do what's required."

Sir Winston Churchill (1874 - 1965), British orator, author and Prime Minister during World War II.

"It's not how big you are, it's how big you play."

John Wooden (1910 - 2010), American Hall of Fame basketball coach for UCLA who won a record 10 NCAA men's championships.

"It's not the hours you put in your work that counts, it's the work you put in the hours."

Sam Ewing (1949 -), American and former major league baseball player.

"It's not the size of the dog in the fight, it's the size of the fight in the dog."

Mark Twain, the pen name of Samuel Langhorne Clemens (1835 – 1910), American writer and humorist.

"It's the little details that are vital. Little things make big things happen."

John Wooden (1910 - 2010), American Hall of Fame basketball coach for UCLA who won a record 10 NCAA men's championships.

"Judge a man by his questions rather than his answers."

Voltaire (1694 - 1778), French writer and philosopher.

"Keep away from people who try to belittle your ambitions. Small people always do that, but the really great make you feel that you, too, can become great."

Mark Twain, the pen name of Samuel Langhorne Clemens (1835 – 1910), American writer and humorist.

"Keep your chin up and you will see the clouds in the sky. Keep your chin down and all you will see is the dirt on the floor."

Shelley L. Young

"Keeping score of old scores and scars, getting even and one-upping, always makes you less than you are."

Malcolm S. Forbes (1919 - 1919), American publisher of *Forbes* magazine.

"Kind words can be short and easy to speak, but their echoes are truly endless."

Mother Teresa (1910 - 1997), Albanian missionary and Nobel Peace Prize winner.

"Kites rise highest against the wind, not with it."

Sir Winston Churchill (1874 - 1965), British orator, author and Prime Minister during World War II.

"Laughing is the sensation of feeling good all over and showing it principally in one spot."

Josh Billings, the pen name of 19th century American humorist Henry Wheeler Shaw (1818 - 1885). He was perhaps the second most famous humor writer and lecturer in the US in the second half of the 19th century after Mark Twain.

"Learn the art of patience. Apply discipline to your thoughts when they become anxious over the outcome of a goal. Impatience breeds anxiety, fear, discouragement and failure. Patience creates confidence, decisiveness, and a rational outlook, which eventually leads to success."

Brian Adams

"Let others lead small lives, but not you. Let others argue over small things, but not you. Let others cry over small hurts, but not you. Let others leave their future in someone else's hands, but not you."

Jim Rohn (1930 - 2009), American entrepreneur, author and motivational speaker. His rags to riches story played a large part in his work, which influenced others in the personal development industry.

"Live with passion!"

Anthony Robbins (1960 -), American self-help author and success coach. His books include *Unlimited Power: The New Science of Personal Achievement* and *Awaken the Giant Within*.

"Losers live in the past. Winners learn from the past and enjoy working in the present toward the future."

Denis Waitley (1933 -), American motivational speaker and writer, consultant and best-selling author.

"Losers make promises they often break. Winners make commitments they always keep."

Denis Waitley (1933 -), American motivational speaker and writer, consultant and best-selling author.

"Luck is preparation meeting opportunity."

Seneca (~ 54 BC - ~ 39 AD), Roman rhetorician and writer.

"May I never miss a sunset or a rainbow because I am looking down."

Sara June Parker

"Mediocre people have an answer for everything and are astonished at nothing."

Eugéne Delacroix (1798 - 1863), French artist.

"Minds, like parachutes, only function when they are open."

Frank Zappa (1940 - 1993), American composer, singer-songwriter, electric guitarist, record producer, and film director.

"Most look up and admire the stars. A champion climbs a mountain and grabs one."

Unknown

"Most people work just hard enough not to get fired and get paid just enough money not to quit."

George Carlin (1937 - 2008), American stand-up comedian, social critic, actor and author, who won five Grammy Awards for his comedy albums.

"Most people would rather be certain they're miserable than risk being happy."

Robert Anthony (1982 -), American professional wrestler.

"My country is the world and my religion is to do good."

Thomas Paine (1737 - 1809), English-born writer and philosopher who played a significant role helping America in the American Revolution.

"Never argue with a stupid person. First they'll drag you down to their level, then they will beat you with experience."

Unknown

"Never give in, never give in, never; never; never; never - in nothing, great or small, large or petty - never give in except to convictions of honor and good sense."

Sir Winston Churchill (1874 - 1965), British orator, author and Prime Minister during World War II.

"Never let the fear of striking out, keep you from playing the game."

Babe Ruth (1895 - 1948), American major league baseball player from 1914 - 1935.

"Never mess up an apology with an excuse."

Unknown

"Never underestimate the power of stupid people in large numbers."

Homer Simpson, *The Simpsons* television show.

"No great deed is done by falterers who ask for certainty."

George Eliot (1819 - 1880), pen name of English writer Mary Ann Evans.

"No one can make you feel inferior without your consent."

Eleanor Roosevelt (1884 - 1962), 32nd US first lady (1933 - 1945), UN diplomat and humanitarian.

"Nothing great was ever achieved without enthusiasm."

Ralph Waldo Emerson (1803 - 1882), American writer and poet.

"Nothing is so contagious as enthusiasm."

Samuel Taylor Coleridge (1772 - 1834), English poet, Romantic, literary critic and philosopher who, with his friend William Wordsworth, was a founder of the Romantic Movement in England and a member of the Lake Poets. He is probably best known for his poems "The Rime of the Ancient Mariner" and "Kubla Khan."

"On no account brood over your wrong-doing. Rolling in the muck is not the best way of getting clean."

Aldous Huxley (1894 - 1963), English writer and author of "Brave New World."

"Once you learn to quit, it becomes a habit."

Vince Lombardi (1913 - 1970), American football coach best known as the head coach of the Green Bay Packers during the 1960s.

"One never knows what each day is going to bring. The important thing is to be open and ready for it."

Henry Moore (1898 - 1986), English sculptor and artist best known for his abstract monumental bronze sculptures which are located around the world as public works of art.

"One of the advantages of being disorderly is that one is constantly making exciting discoveries."

A. A. Milne (1882 - 1956), English author, best known for his books about the teddy bear Winnie-the-Pooh and for various children's poems.

"One person with a belief is worth 99 people who have only interests."

Dale Carnegie (1888 - 1955), American writer, lecturer, and the developer of famous courses in self-improvement, salesmanship, corporate training, public speaking, and interpersonal skills. He's best known as author of "How to Win Friends and Influence People" (1936).

"Only the mediocre are always at their best."

Jean Giraudoux (1882 - 1944), French novelist, essayist, diplomat and playwright.

"Only those who dare to fail greatly can ever achieve greatly."

Robert F. Kennedy (1925 - 1968), American politician, a Democratic senator from New York, and a noted civil rights activist. An icon of modern American liberalism and member of the Kennedy family, he was a younger brother of President John F. Kennedy and acted as one of his advisors during his presidency. From 1961 to 1964, he was the US Attorney General.

"Our attitude toward life determines life's attitude towards us."

John N. Mitchell

"Our doubts are traitors, and make us lose the good we oft might win, by fearing to attempt."

William Shakespeare (1564 - 1616), one of England's greatest playwrights.

"Our limitations and success will be based, most often, on your own expectations for ourselves. What the mind dwells upon, the body acts upon."

Denis Waitley (1933 -), American motivational speaker and writer, consultant and best-selling author.

"Our lives begin to end, the day we become silent, about things that matter."

Martin Luther King Jr. (1929 - 1968), American civil rights leader and Nobel Peace Prize winner.

"Our lives improve only when we take chances -- and the first and most difficult risk we can take is to be honest with ourselves."

Walter Anderson

"Pain is inevitable in life, but suffering is not. How you cope determines that."

Dr. Mehmet Oz (1960 -), a Turkish-American cardiothoracic surgeon, author, and host and commentator for the syndicated daily television program focusing on medical issues/personal health, *The Dr. Oz Show*.

"Pain is temporary...quitting is forever."

Lance Armstrong (1971 -), American cyclist, 7-time winner of the Tour de France, cancer survivor.

"People are always blaming their circumstances for what they are. I don't believe in circumstances. The people who get on in this world are the people who get up and look for the circumstances they want, and if they can't find them, they make them."

George Bernard Shaw (1856 - 1950), Irish writer and playwright who won the 1925 Nobel Prize for Literature.

"People are best convinced by things they themself discover."

Benjamin Franklin (1706 - 1790), American statesman, scientist, writer and printer.

"People who are unable to motivate themselves must be content with mediocrity, no matter how impressive their other talents."

Andrew Carnegie, (1835-1919), Scottish-born American industrialist and philanthropist.

"People who say it cannot be done should not interrupt those who are doing it."

Hilary Young

"People would worry less about what others think of them if they only realized how seldom they do."

Unknown

"Perseverance is not a long race. It is many short races one after another."

Walter Elliott (1842 - 1928), American Roman Catholic priest and missionary. From "The Spiritual Life."

"Perseverance is the hard work you do after you get tired of doing the hard work you already did."

Newt Gingrich (1943 -), American politician who served as the 58th Speaker of the United States House of Representatives (1995 - 1999).

"Persistence isn't using the same tactics over and over. That's just annoying. Persistence is having the same goal over and over."

Seth Godin (1960 -), American entrepreneur, author and public speaker. Godin popularized the topic of permission marketing.

"Practice isn't the thing you do once you're good. It's the thing you do that makes you good."

Malcolm Gladwell (1963 -), Canadian journalist.

"Press on. Nothing in the world can take the place of Persistence. Talent will not; nothing is more common than unsuccessful men with talent. Genius will not; unrewarded genius is almost a proverb. Education will not; the world is full of educated derelicts. Persistence and determination alone are omnipotent."

Calvin Coolidge (1872 - 1933), 30th US President (1923- 1929).

"Pretend that every single person you meet has a sign around his or her neck that says, 'Make me feel important.'"

Mary Kay Ash (1918 - 2001), American businesswoman and Founder of Mary Kay Cosmetics.

"Problems are not stop signs, they are guidelines."

Robert Schuller (1926 -), American televangelist, pastor, and author known principally through the weekly "Hour of Power" television broadcast that he began in 1970.

"Progress always involves risk; you can't steal second base and keep your foot on first base."

Frederick Wilcox

"Relentless, repetitive self talk is what changes our self-image."

Denis Waitley (1933 -), American motivational speaker and writer, consultant and best-selling author.

"Research is to see what everybody else has seen, and to think what nobody else has thought."

Albert Szent-Györgi (1893 - 1986), Hungarian physiologist who won the Nobel Prize in Medicine in 1937 and is credited with discovering vitamin C.

"Resentment is like drinking poison and waiting for the other person to die."

Carrie Fischer (1956 -), American novelist, screenwriter, actress and lecturer most famous for her portrayal of Princess Leia Organa in the original *Star Wars* movie trilogy.

"Risks, I like to say, always pay off. You learn what to do, or what not to do."

Jonas Salk, (1914 - 1995), American biologist. Developed the vaccine for polio.

"Serenity is not freedom from the storm, but peace among it."

Unknown

"Sing like nobody's listening, dance like nobody's watching, love like you've never been hurt, and live like it's heaven on earth."

Mark Twain, the pen name of Samuel Langhorne Clemens (1835 – 1910), American writer and humorist.

"Skate to where the puck is."

Wayne Gretzky (1961 -), Canadian professional ice hockey player considered to be the best who ever played the game.

"Smile.... it makes others wonder what you're thinking."

Unknown

"Smile when it hurts most."

Unknown

"Some of the world's greatest feats were accomplished by people not smart enough to know they were impossible."

Doug Larson (1926 -), American syndicated newspaper columnist.

"Sometimes doing your best is not good enough. Sometimes you must do what is required."

Sir Winston Churchill (1874 - 1965), British orator, author and Prime Minister during World War II.

"Sometimes we must get hurt in order to grow. We must fail in order to know. Sometimes our vision is clear only after our eyes are washed away with tears."

Unknown

"Speak when you are angry - and you'll make the best speech you'll ever regret."

Dr. Laurence J. Peter (1919 - 1990), Canadian educator and "hierarchiologist", best known to the general public for the formulation of the Peter Principle.

"Start by doing what is necessary, then do what is possible, and suddenly you are doing the impossible."

Saint Francis of Assisi (1182 - 1226), Italian friar and Founder of the Franciscan Order.

"Strategy is the big picture, the distant outcome. People who operate from a strategic base think in larger terms, have grander visions and demand more of themselves and their lives. They discover order where others see only chaos, significance where others find only coincidence."

Shale Paul

"Surround yourself with only people who are going to lift you higher."

Oprah Winfrey (1954 -), American television host, actress, producer, and philanthropist, best known for her self-titled, multi-award winning talk show, which has become the highest-rated program of its kind in history. She has been ranked the richest African American of the 20th century, the greatest black philanthropist in American history, and was once the world's only black billionaire. She is also, according to some assessments, the most influential woman in the world.

"Tact is the art of making a point without making an enemy."

Sir Isaac Newton (1643 - 1727), English physicist, mathematician, astronomer, natural philosopher, alchemist, and theologian. His "Philosophiæ Naturalis Principia Mathematica" (Latin for "Mathematical Principles of Natural Philosophy"; usually called the *Principia*), published in 1687, is one of the most important scientific books ever written.

"Take charge of your attitude. Don't let someone else choose it for you."

Unknown

"Take risks: if you win, you will be happy; if you lose, you will be wise."

Unknown

"Talent is God given. Be humble. Fame is man-given. Be grateful. Conceit is self-given. Be careful."

John Wooden (1910 - 2010), American Hall of Fame basketball coach for UCLA who won a record 10 NCAA men's championships.

"The art of conversation is not only to say the right thing at the right time, but also to leave unsaid, the wrong thing at the most tempting moment."

Dee Tenori

"The best thing to give your enemy is forgiveness; to an opponent, tolerance; to a friend, your heart; to your child, a good example; to a father, deference; to your mother, conduct that will make her proud of you; to yourself, respect; to all men, charity."

Francis Maitland Balfour (1851 - 1882), British biologist.

"The big rewards come to those who travel the second, undemanded mile."

Bruce Barton (1886 - 1967), American advertising executive and US congressman.

"The brain is a wonderful organ. It starts working the moment you get up in the morning and does not stop until you get into the office."

Robert Frost (1874 - 1963), American poet.

"The Chinese use two brush strokes to write the word 'crisis.' One brush stroke stands for danger; the other for opportunity. In a crisis, be aware of the danger - but recognize the opportunity."

John F. Kennedy (1917 - 1963), 35th US President (1961 - 1963).

"The control center of your life is your attitude."

Norman Cousins (1915 - 1990), American political journalist, author, professor, and world peace advocate.

"The conventional view serves to protect us from the painful job of thinking."

John Kenneth Galbraith (1908 - 2006), Canadian-American economist. He was a Keynesian and an Institutionalist, a leading proponent of 20th-century political liberalism.

"The cure for boredom is curiosity. There is no cure for curiosity."

Dorothy Parker (1893 - 1967), American short-story writer and poet.

"The difficult is what takes a little time; the impossible is what takes a little longer."

Fridtjof Nansen (1861–1930), Norwegian explorer and Nobel Prize Winner.

"The first quality that is needed is audacity."

Sir Winston Churchill (1874 - 1965), British orator, author and Prime Minister during World War II.

"The first step in solving a problem is to recognize that you have a problem."

Unknown

"The greatest mistake you can make in life is to be continually fearing you will make one."

Elbert Hubbard (1856 - 1915), American writer and editor.

"The harder I work, the luckier I get."

Lee Trevino (1939 -), American professional golfer.

"The least initial deviation from the truth is multiplied later a thousand fold."

Aristotle (384 - 322 BC), Greek writer, teacher and philosopher, often considered the father of logic.

"The longer I live, the more I realize the impact of attitude on life. Attitude, to me, is more important than facts. It is more important than the past, the education, the money, than circumstances, than failure, than successes, than what other people think or say or do. It is more important than appearance, giftedness or skill. It will make or break a company... a church... a home. The remarkable thing is we have a choice everyday regarding the attitude we will embrace for that day. We cannot change our past... we cannot change the fact that people will act in a certain way. We cannot change the inevitable. The only thing we can do is play on the one string we have, and that is our attitude. I am convinced that life is 10% what happens to me and 90% of how I react to it. And so it is with you... we are in charge of our attitudes."

Charles R. Swindoll (1934 -), American evangelical Christian pastor, author, educator and radio preacher.

"The main thing is to keep the main thing the main thing."

Zig Ziglar (1926 -), American author, salesman, and motivational speaker.

"The man who has confidence in himself gains the confidence of others."

Hasidic saying.

"The more passions and desires one has, the more ways one has of being happy."

Charlotte-Catherine

"The only people with whom you should try to get even are those who have helped you."

John E. Southard

"The only person you are destined to become is the person you decide to be."

Ralph Waldo Emerson (1803 - 1882), American writer and poet.

"The only way to find the limits of the possible is by going beyond them to the impossible."

Sir Arthur C. Clarke (1917 - 2008), British science fiction author, inventor, and futurist most famous for the novel "2001: A Space Odyssey."

"The opposite of courage in our society is not cowardice, it is conformity."

Rollo May (1909 - 1994), American existential psychologist.

"The person who knows how to laugh at himself will never cease to be amused."

Shirley MacLaine (1934 -), outspoken American actress and dancer.

"The power of accurate observation is commonly called cynicism by those who have not got it."

George Bernard Shaw (1856 - 1950), Irish writer and playwright who won the 1925 Nobel Prize for Literature.

"The reasonable man adapts himself to the world; the unreasonable one persists in trying to adapt the world to himself. Therefore all progress depends on the unreasonable man."

George Bernard Shaw (1856 - 1950), Irish writer and playwright who won the 1925 Nobel Prize for Literature. From 1903 play "Man and Superman."

"The secret of health for both mind and body is not to mourn for the past, not to worry about the future, or not to anticipate troubles, but to live the present moment wisely and earnestly."

Gautama Buddha, a spiritual teacher who founded Buddhism.

"The significance of a new idea is directly proportional to the resistance to it."

Unknown

"The single biggest problem in communication is the illusion that it has taken place."

George Bernard Shaw (1856 - 1950), Irish writer and playwright who won the 1925 Nobel Prize for Literature.

"The squeaking wheel doesn't always get the grease. Sometimes it gets replaced."

Vic Gold (1928 -), American journalist, author, and Republican political consultant. His career as a political consultant spanned the period from the 1964 Presidential candidacy of Barry Goldwater through George H. W. Bush's 1992 re-election campaign, and he co-wrote Bush's 1987 autobiography.

"The Three Rules of Work: '1. Out of clutter, find simplicity. 2. From discord, find harmony. 3. In the middle of difficulty lies opportunity.'"

Albert Einstein (1879 - 1955), German-born American physicist who developed the theories of relativity and won the Nobel Prize for Physics in 1921.

"The time is now, the place is here. Stay in the present. You can do nothing to change the past, and the future will never come exactly as you plan or hope for."

Dan Millman (1946 -), former Trampolining world champion athlete, university coach, martial arts instructor and college professor, and an author of fourteen self-help books, currently published in 29 languages, the most famous of which is the semi-autobiographical novel, "Way of the Peaceful Warrior" (1980), which was adapted into a feature film, *Peaceful Warrior* (2006) starring Nick Nolte.

"The trouble with ignorance is that it picks up confidence as it goes along."

Arnold Glasow

"The truth is incontrovertible, malice may attack it, ignorance may deride it, but in the end; there it is."

Sir Winston Churchill (1874 - 1965), British orator, author and Prime Minister during World War II.

"The truth is, creativity isn't about wild talent as much as it's about productivity. To find a few ideas that work, you need to try a lot that don't. It's a pure numbers game."

Robert Sutton, a Professor of Management Science and Engineering at Stanford University's Engineering School.

"The winner's edge is not in a gifted birth, a high IQ, or in talent. The winner's edge is all in the attitude, not aptitude. Attitude is the criterion for success."

Denis Waitley (1933 -), American motivational speaker and writer, consultant and best-selling author.

"There are times when forgetting can be just as important as remembering - and even more difficult."

Unknown

"There is no effective competition against exceptional quality service."

Unknown

"There is nothing worse than aggressive stupidity."

Johann Wolfgang von Goethe (1749 - 1832), German writer, philosopher and scientist.

"There is nothing to be gained by second guessing yourself, you can't remake the past. Look forward or risk being left behind."

Unknown

"Things work out best for people who work best with how things work out."

Unknown

"Those that think it permissible to tell white lies soon grow color blind."

Austin O'Malley

"To hate a person is a waste; half the people you hate don't care, and the other half don't know."

Unknown

"To make mistakes is human; to stumble is commonplace; to be able to laugh at yourself is maturity."

William Arthur Ward (1921 - 1994), American writer of inspirational articles, poems and meditations.

"To strive, to seek, to find, and not to yield!"

Lord Alfred Tennyson (1809 - 1892), English poet.

"Too many people guess with unwarranted confidence or offer ill-informed opinions. There is no shame in listening or saying 'I don't know, but I'll find out.'"

Unknown

"Tough times don't last but, tough people do!"

Unknown

"True genius resides in the capacity for evaluation of uncertain, hazardous, and conflicting opinions."

Sir Winston Churchill (1874 - 1965), British orator, author and Prime Minister during World War II.

"Trust yourself. Create the kind of self that you will be happy to live with all your life. Make the most of yourself by fanning the tiny, inner sparks of possibility into flames of achievement."

Golda Meir (1898 - 1978), a teacher, kibbutznik and politician who became the fourth Prime Minister of the State of Israel.

"Undoubtedly, we become what we envisage."

Claude M. Bristol

"Unless a man feels he has a good memory, he should never venture to lie."

Michel de Montaigne (1533 - 1592), one of the most influential writers of the French Renaissance, known for popularizing the essay as a literary genre and is popularly thought of as the father of Modern Skepticism.

"Unthinking respect for authority is the greatest enemy of truth."

Albert Einstein (1879 - 1955), German-born American physicist who developed the theories of relativity and won the Nobel Prize for Physics in 1921.

"Vitality shows not only the ability to persist, but in the ability to start over."

F. Scott Fitzgerald (1896 - 1940), American novelist.

"Walk the words you talk and talk the words you walk."

Unknown

"We all get what we tolerate."

Unknown

"We are not permitted to choose the frame of our destiny. But what we put into it is ours."

Dag Hammarskjold (1905 - 1961), Swedish diplomat, economist and Nobel Prize winner.

"We are what we repeatedly do. Excellence, therefore, is not an act but a habit."

Aristotle (384 BC - 322 BC), Greek writer, teacher and philosopher, often considered the father of logic.

"We cannot banish dangers, but we can banish fears."

David Sarnoff (1891 - 1971), American businessman and pioneer of American commercial radio and television. He became President of RCA and NBC.

"We cannot become what we need to be by remaining what we are."

Max DePree, American writer and businessman.

"We don't stop playing because we grow old; we grow old because we stop playing."

George Bernard Shaw (1856 - 1950), Irish writer and playwright who won the 1925 Nobel Prize for Literature.

"We don't want a thing because we have found a reason for it - we find a reason for it because we want it."

Unknown

"We gain strength, and courage, and confidence by each experience in which we really stop to look fear in the face... we must do that which we think we cannot."

Eleanor Roosevelt (1884 - 1962), 32nd US first lady (1933 - 1945), UN diplomat and humanitarian.

"We have two ears and one mouth so that we can listen twice as much as we speak."

Epictetus (55 AD - 135 AD), Greek Stoic philosopher.

"We usually overestimate what we think we can accomplish in one year; but we grossly underestimate what we can accomplish in a decade."

Anthony Robbins (1960 -), American self-help author and success coach. His books include "Unlimited Power: The New Science of Personal Achievement" and "Awaken the Giant Within."

"What lies before us and what lies behind us are tiny matters compared to what lies within us."

Ralph Waldo Emerson (1803 - 1882), American writer and poet.

"What others think of us would be of little moment did it not, when known, so deeply tinge what we think of ourselves."

Paul Valery (1871 - 1945), French poet, essayist, and philosopher.

"What we must decide is how we are valuable rather than how valuable we are."

F. Scott Fitzgerald (1896 - 1940), American novelist.

"What we obtain too cheaply we esteem too little; it is dearness only that gives everything its value."

Thomas Paine (1737 - 1809), English-born writer and philosopher who played a significant role helping America in the American Revolution.

"Whatever course you decide upon, there is always someone to tell you that you are wrong. There are always difficulties arising which tempt you to believe that your critics are right. To map out a course of action and follow it to an end requires courage."

Ralph Waldo Emerson (1803 - 1882), American writer and poet.

"When a person shows you who they are, believe them the first time."

Maya Angelou (1928 -), American author and poet.

"When a person wants to believe something, it doesn't take much to convince them."

Unknown

"When faced with a challenge, look for a way, not a way out."

David Weatherford

"When the going gets tough, the tough get going."

English proverb.

"When we are dreaming alone it is only a dream. When we are dreaming with others, it is the beginning of reality."

Dom Helder Camara, (1909 - 1999), Brazilian Roman Catholic Archbishop.

"When you are trying to convince yourself something is right, it is usually wrong."

Unknown

"When you hold resentment toward another, you are bound to that person or condition by an emotional link that is stronger than steel. Forgiveness is the only way to dissolve that link and get free."

Catherine Ponder (1927 -), American minister and inspirational author.

"When you know what you want, and want it bad enough, you will find a way to get it."

Jim Rohn (1930 - 2009), American entrepreneur, author and motivational speaker. His rags to riches story played a large part in his work, which influenced others in the personal development industry.

"When you make a mistake, there are only three things you should ever do about it: admit it, learn from it, and do not repeat it."

Paul "Bear" Bryant (1913 - 1983), American college football coach best known as the longtime head coach at the University of Alabama.

"When you stop drinking, you have to deal with this marvelous personality that started you drinking in the first place."

Jimmy Breslin (1930 -), American journalist and author.

"When you consistently maintain a positive frame of mind, you'll become known as a problem-solver rather than a complainer. People avoid complainers. They seek out problem-solvers."

Joseph Sommerville

"When you think of the long and gloomy history of man, you will find more hideous crimes have been committed in the name of obedience than have ever been committed in the name of rebellion."

C.P. Snow (1905 - 1980), English physicist and novelist who also served in several important positions with the UK government.

"Whenever you are asked if you can do a job, tell 'em, 'Certainly, I can!' Then get busy and find out how to do it."

Theodore Roosevelt (1858 - 1919), 26th US President (1901 - 1909).

"Whenever you're in conflict with someone, there is one factor that can make the difference between damaging your relationship and deepening it. That factor is attitude."

William James (1842 - 1910), a pioneering American psychologist and philosopher who was trained as a medical doctor. He wrote influential books on the young science of psychology, educational psychology, psychology of religious experience and mysticism, and on the philosophy of pragmatism.

"Whether you think you can or whether you think you can't, you're right."

Henry Ford (1863 - 1947), prominent American industrialist, the founder of the Ford Motor Company, and sponsor of the development of the assembly line technique of mass production.

"Who wants a dream that's near-fetched?"

Howard Schultz (1953 -), American entrepreneur and Chairman of Starbucks.

"Why do we fear adversity, when we know that overcoming it is the only way to become stronger, smarter, and better?"

John Wooden (1910 - 2010), American Hall of Fame basketball coach for UCLA who won a record 10 NCAA men's championships.

"Winners have the ability to step back from the canvas of their lives like an artist gaining perspective. They make their lives a work of art / an individual masterpiece."

Denis Waitley (1933 -), American motivational speaker and writer, consultant and best-selling author.

"Winners take time to relish their work, knowing that scaling the mountain is what makes the view from the top so exhilarating."

Denis Waitley (1933 -), American motivational speaker and writer, consultant and best-selling author.

"Winning isn't everything - but wanting to win is."

Vince Lombardi (1913 - 1970), American football coach best known as the head coach of the Green Bay Packers during the 1960s.

"Wise men put their trust in ideas and not in circumstances."

Ralph Waldo Emerson (1803 - 1882), American writer and poet.

"Without deviation from the norm, progress is not possible."

Frank Zappa (1940 - 1993), American composer, singer-songwriter, electric guitarist, record producer, and film director.

"Without passion, you don't have energy; without energy, you have nothing. Nothing great in the world has been accomplished without passion."

Donald Trump (1946 -), American business magnate, socialite, author, and television personality.

"Women who seek to be equal with men lack ambition."

Timothy Leary (1920 - 1996), a highly influential American psychologist and writer, known in later life for advocating advanced research into the therapeutic benefits of psychedelic drugs.

"Work expands so as to fill the time available for its completion."

Parkinson's Law

"Work in a way that has your employer continually thinking of ways to keep you rather than reasons to keep you."

Sam Parker (1965 -), Co-Founder of JustSell, a website focused on sales success.

"Work like you don't need the money. Love like you've never been hurt. Dance like nobody's watching."

Leroy Robert "Satchel" Paige (1906 - 1983), pitcher for the Pittsburgh Crawfords and the Kansas City Monarchs of the Negro Leagues; Cleveland Indians, St. Louis Browns and Kansas City Athletics of MLB (1926-53, 1965), Hall of Fame (1971).

"Years may wrinkle the skin, but lack of enthusiasm wrinkles the soul."

Unknown

"Yes We Can."

President Barack H. Obama (1961 -), American, 44th US President and first African-American President.

"You are not what you think you are, you are not what others think you are, you are what you think others think you are."

Unknown

"You are now at a crossroads. This is your opportunity to make the most important decision you will ever make. Forget your past. Who are you now? Who have you decided you really are now? Don't think about who you have been. Who are you now? Who have you decided to become? Make this decision consciously. Make it carefully. Make it powerfully."

Anthony Robbins (1960 -), American self-help author and success coach. His books include *Unlimited Power: The New Science of Personal Achievement* and *Awaken the Giant Within*.

"You are the only person on earth who can use your ability."

Zig Ziglar (1926 -), American author, salesman, and motivational speaker.

"You are today where your thoughts have brought you; you will be tomorrow where your thoughts take you."

James Lane Allen (1849 - 1925), American novelist and short story writer.

"You can gain more friends by being yourself than you can by putting up a front. You can gain more friends by building people up than you can by tearing them down. And you can gain more friends by taking a few minutes from each day to do something kind for someone, whether it be a friend or a complete stranger. What a difference one person can make!"

Sasha Azevedo, American actress, athlete and model.

"You can tell whether a man is clever by his answers. You can tell whether a man is wise by his questions."

Naguib Mahfouz (1911 -), Egyptian novelist and screenplay writer who won the 1988 Nobel Prize for Literature.

"You cannot change your destination overnight, but you can change your direction overnight."

Jim Rohn (1930 - 2009), American entrepreneur, author and motivational speaker. His rags to riches story played a large part in his work, which influenced others in the personal development industry.

"You cannot control what happens to you, but you can control your attitude toward what happens to you, and in that, you will be mastering change rather than allowing it to master you."

Brian Tracy (1944 -), Canadian self-help author who has recorded many of his works as audio books. His presentations and seminar topics include leadership, sales, managerial effectiveness, and business strategy.

"You cannot kindle a fire in any other heart until it is burning in your own."

Unknown

"You cannot talk yourself out of a situation you have yourself behaved into."

Stephen R. Covey (1932 -), Professor and author best known for the best-selling book, "The Seven Habits of Highly Effective People."

"You can't let praise or criticism get to you. It's a weakness to get caught up in either one."

John Wooden (1910 - 2010), American Hall of Fame basketball coach for UCLA who won a record 10 NCAA men's championships.

"You can't live a perfect day without doing something for someone who will never be able to repay you."

John Wooden (1910 - 2010), American Hall of Fame basketball coach for UCLA who won a record 10 NCAA men's championships.

"You can't soar like an eagle when you are flying with turkeys."

Unknown

"You don't get paid for the hour. You get paid for the value you bring to the hour."

Jim Rohn (1930 - 2009), American entrepreneur, author and motivational speaker. His rags to riches story played a large part in his work, which influenced others in the personal development industry.

"You have brains in your head. You have feet in your shoes. You can steer yourself any direction you choose. You're out on your own. And you know what you know. And YOU are the one who'll decide where to go..."

Dr. Seuss (1904 - 1991), the penname of Theodor Geisel, American writer and cartoonist most widely known for his children's books.

"You have to find something that you love enough to be able to take risks, jump over the hurdles and break through the brick walls that are always going to be placed in front of you."

George Lucas (1944 -), creator of the epic "Star Wars" movie series.

"You have to have confidence in your ability, and then be tough enough to follow through."

Rosalynn Carter (1927 -), American and wife of the former President of the United States Jimmy Carter and in that capacity served as the First Lady of the United States from 1977 to 1981. As First Lady and after, she has been a leading advocate for numerous causes, perhaps most prominently for mental health research.

"You learn something every day if you pay attention."

Ray LeBlond

"You may be deceived if you trust too much, but you will live in torment if you do not trust enough."

Frank Crane (1873 - 1948), American stage and film actor and director.

"You miss 100% of the shots you never take."

Wayne Gretzky (1961 -), Canadian professional ice hockey player considered to be the best who ever played the game.

"You need to suspend disbelief to start a company. So many people will tell you that what you're doing can't be done."

Paul Maeder, American venture capitalist at Highland Capital Partners.

"You never get a second chance to make a good first impression."

Will Rogers (1879 -1935), Cherokee-American cowboy, social commentator.

"You only get to be victim once. After that, you're a volunteer."

Naomi Judd (1946 -), American country music singer, songwriter, and activist.

"You see things and you say, 'Why?' but I dream things that never were and I say 'Why not?'"

George Bernard Shaw (1856 - 1950), Irish writer and playwright who won the 1925 Nobel Prize for Literature.

"Your attitude, not your aptitude, will determine your altitude."

Zig Ziglar (1926 -), American author, salesman, and motivational speaker.

"Your living is determined not so much by what life brings to you as by the attitude you bring to life; not so much by what happens to you as by the way your mind looks at what happens."

Kahil Gibran (1883 - 1931), Lebanese-born American philosophical essayist, novelist and poet.

"Your present circumstances don't determine where you can go; they merely determine where you start."

Nino Qubein

"Your true value depends entirely on what you are compared with."

Bob Wells, American editor for *Windows and .NET* magazine.

"You've got to cross the line every once in a while to know where it is."

Sam Parker (1965 -), Co-Founder of *JustSell*, a website focused on sales success.

"You've got to get up every morning with determination if you're going to go to bed with satisfaction."

George Horace Lorimer (1867 - 1937), American journalist and author. He is best known as the editor of The *Saturday Evening Post*.

change

accept attitude business **change** control decisions
discomforts dollars doors drawbacks family fear history impact irrelevance life
peak performers perspective regret speed stubbornness

"Any change, even a change for the better, is always accompanied by drawbacks and discomforts."

Arnold Bennett (1867 - 1931), English novelist.

"Be the change you want to see in the world."

Mahatma Gandhi (1869 - 1948), a pre-eminent political and ideological leader of India during the Indian independence movement.

"Change has a considerable psychological impact on the human mind. To the fearful it is threatening because it means that things may get worse. To the hopeful it is encouraging because things may get better. To the confident it is inspiring because the challenge exists to make things better."

King Whitney Jr.

"Change is good, but dollars are better."

Unknown

"Change is not merely necessary to life - it is life."

Alvin Toffler (1928 -), American writer and futurist.

"Change is the essence of life. Be willing to surrender what you are for what you could become."

Unknown

"Change is the law of life. And those who look only to the past or present are certain to miss the future."

John F. Kennedy (1917 - 1963), 35th US President (1961 - 1963).

"Change what you cannot accept and accept what you cannot change."

Unknown

"Consider how hard it is to change yourself; and you will understand what little chance you have trying to change others."

Unknown

"Do one thing every day that scares you."

Eleanor Roosevelt (1884 - 1962), 32nd US first lady (1933 - 1945), UN diplomat and humanitarian.

"Even though we've changed and we're all finding our own place in the world, we all know that when the tears fall or the smile spreads across our face, we'll come to each other because no matter where this crazy world takes us, nothing will ever change so much to the point where we're not all still friends."

Unknown

"Few will have the greatness to bend history itself; but each of us can work to change a small portion of events, and in the total of all those acts will be written the history of this generation."

Robert F. Kennedy (1925 - 1968), American politician, a Democratic senator from New York, and a noted civil rights activist. An icon of modern American liberalism and member of the Kennedy family, he was a younger brother of President John F. Kennedy and acted as one of his advisors during his presidency. From 1961 to 1964, he was the US Attorney General.

"I find it fascinating that most people plan their vacations with better care than they plan their lives. Perhaps that is because escape is easier than change."

Jim Rohn (1930 - 2009), American entrepreneur, author and motivational speaker. His rags to riches story played a large part in his work, which influenced others in the personal development industry.

"If things seem under control, you're just not going fast enough."

Mario Andretti (1940 -), retired Italian-American world champion racing driver, one of the most successful Americans in the history of the sport.

"If you always do what you always did, you'll always get what you always got."

Mark Twain, the pen name of Samuel Langhorne Clemens (1835 – 1910), American writer and humorist.

"If you don't like change, you're going to like irrelevance even less."

General Eric Shinseki (1942 -), former US Army Chief of Staff and current US Secretary of Veterans Affairs.

"If you don't like something about yourself, change it. If you can't change it, accept it."

Ted Shackelford (1946 -), American actor.

"In embracing change, entrepreneurs ensure social and economic stability."

George Gilder (1939 -), American writer, techno-utopian intellectual, Republican Party activist, and co-founder of the Discovery Institute.

"It is better to regret something you did, rather than to regret something you didn't do."

Unknown

"None of us knows what the next change is going to be, what unexpected opportunity is just around the corner, waiting a few months or a few years to change all the tenor of our lives."

Kathleen Norris (1880 - 1966), American novelist.

"Not everything that is faced can be changed, but nothing can be changed until it is faced."

James Baldwin (1924 - 1987), American novelist, writer, playwright, poet, essayist and civil rights activist.

"One cannot manage change. One can only be ahead of it."

Peter F. Drucker (1909 - 2006), American writer and management consultant.

"Other things may change us, but we start and end with family."

Anthony Brandt

"Peak performers see the ability to manage change as a necessity in fulfilling their missions."

Charles Garfield

"Sometimes it's the smallest decisions that can change your life forever."

Keri Russell (1976 -), American actress and dancer. After appearing in a number of made-for-television films and series during the mid-1990s, she came to fame for portraying the title role of Felicity Porter on the series *Felicity*, which ran from 1998 to 2002, and for which she won a Golden Globe Award. Russell has since appeared in several films, including *We Were Soldiers, The Upside of Anger, Mad About Mambo, Wonder Woman, Mission: Impossible III, Waitress, August Rush, Bedtime Stories*, and *Extraordinary Measures*.

"The doors we open and close each day decide the lives we live."

Flora Whittemore

"The easiest thing to be in the world is you. The most difficult thing to be is what other people want you to be. Don't let them put you in that position."

Leo Buscaglia (1924 - 1998), American author, motivational speaker, and a professor in the Department of Special Education at the University of Southern California.

"The key to change... is to let go of fear."

Roseanne Cash (1955 -), American singer-songwriter and author. She is the eldest daughter of the late country music singer Johnny Cash and his first wife, Vivian Liberto Cash Distin.

"The only difference between a rut and a grave is their dimensions."

Ellen Glasgow (1873 - 1945), Pulitzer Prize-winning American novelist who portrayed the changing world of the contemporary South.

"The only way to make sense out of change is to plunge into it, move with it, and join the dance."

Alan Watts (1915 - 1973), British philosopher, writer, and speaker, best known as an interpreter and popularizer of Eastern philosophy for a Western audience.

"The world is moving so fast these days that the man who says it cannot be done is generally interrupted by someone doing it."

Elbert Hubbard (1856 - 1915), American writer and editor.

"This is a fantastic time to be entering the business world, because business is going to change more in the next 10 years than it has in the last 50."

Bill Gates (1955 -), American business magnate, philanthropist, author best known for Co-Founding software giant Microsoft.

"We must always change, renew, rejuvenate ourselves; otherwise we harden."

Johann Wolfgang von Goethe (1749 - 1832), German writer, philosopher and scientist.

"When you change the way you look at things, the things you look at change."

Dr. Wayne W. Dyer (1940 -), American self-help advocate, author, and lecturer.

"When you're finished changing, you're finished."

Benjamin Franklin (1706 - 1790), American statesman, scientist, writer and printer.

"Yes, there are two paths you can go by / But in the long run / There's still time to change the road you're on."

Lyric from *Led Zeppelin* song "Stairway to Heaven."

"You are educated. Your certification is in your degree. You may think of it as the ticket to the good life. Let me ask you to think of an alternative. Think of it as your ticket to change."

Tom Brokaw (1940 -), American television journalist and author best known as the anchor and managing editor of *NBC Nightly News* from 1982 to 2004. He is the author of "The Greatest Generation" (1998) and other books and the recipient of numerous awards and honors.

character

actions adversity ambition challenge

compromise controversy failure honesty humor integrity laughter lies personality

reputation soul success thoughts truth value words

"A man never discloses his own character so clearly as when he describes another's."

Jean Paul Richter (1763 - 1825), German novelist and humorist.

"A signature always reveals a man's character... and sometimes even his name."

Evan Esar (1899 - 1995), American humorist.

"Adversity doesn't build character, it reveals it."

Unknown

"Any fool can criticize, condemn, and complain but it takes character and self control to be understanding and forgiving."

Dale Carnegie (1888 - 1955), American writer, lecturer, and the developer of famous courses in self-improvement, salesmanship, corporate training, public speaking, and interpersonal skills. He's best known as author of "How to Win Friends and Influence People" (1936).

"Be bold in what you stand for; and careful what you fall for."

Ruth Boorstin, American writer and poet.

"Be more concerned with your character than your reputation, because your character is what you really are, while your reputation is merely what others think you are."

John Wooden (1910 - 2010), American Hall of Fame basketball coach for UCLA who won a record 10 NCAA men's championships.

"Be yourself. Everyone else is already taken."

James Joyce (1882 - 1941), Irish novelist and poet, considered to be one of the most influential writers in the modernist avant-garde of the early 20th century. Joyce is best known for "Ulysses" (1922), a landmark novel which perfected his stream of consciousness technique and combined nearly every literary device available in a modern re-telling of "The Odyssey."

"Champions do not become champions when they win the event, but in the hours, weeks, months and years they spend preparing for it. The victorious performance itself is merely the demonstration of their championship character."

T. Alan Armstrong

"Character cannot be developed in ease and in quiet. Only through the experience of trial and suffering can the soul be strengthened, ambition inspired and success achieved."

Helen Keller (1880 - 1968), American author, political activist, and lecturer. She was the first deafblind person to earn a Bachelor of Arts degree. The story of how Keller's teacher, Anne Sullivan, broke through the isolation imposed by a near complete lack of language, allowing the girl to blossom as she learned to communicate, has become widely known through the dramatic depictions of the play and film "The Miracle Worker."

"Character develops itself in the stream of life."

Johann Wolfgang von Goethe (1749 - 1832), German writer, philosopher and scientist.

"Character is a journey, not a destination."

Bill Clinton (1946 -), American, 42nd US President (1993 - 2001).

"Character is like a tree and reputation like a shadow. The shadow is what we think of it; the tree is the real thing."

Abraham Lincoln (1809 - 1865), 16th US President. His term of office was from 1861 to 1865 and included the American Civil War.

"Character is like the foundation of a house - it is below the surface."

Unknown

"Character is long-standing habit."

Plutarch (46 AD - 119 AD), Ancient Greek biographer and author.

"Character is made by what you stand for; reputation, by what you fall for."

Robert Quillen (1887 - 1948), American journalist and humorist.

"Character is so largely affected by association, that we cannot afford to be indifferent as to who or what our friends are."

Unknown

"Character is the firm foundation stone upon which one must build to win respect. Just as no worthy building can be erected on a weak foundation, so no lasting reputation worthy of respect can be built on a weak character."

R.C. Samsel

"Character is the result of two things: mental attitude and the way we spend our time."

Elbert Hubbard (1856 - 1915), American writer and editor.

"Character is what you know you are, not what others think you have."

Unknown

"Character is what you are. Reputation is what people think you are."

Henry H. Saunderson

"Character, in the long run, is the decisive factor in the life of an individual and of nations alike."

Theodore Roosevelt (1858 - 1919), 26th US President (1901 - 1909).

"Do the right thing even when no one is looking."

Unknown

"Every man has three characters - that which he exhibits, that which he has, and that which he thinks he has."

Jean-Baptiste Alphonse Karr (1808 - 1890), French critic, journalist, and novelist.

"Good character is more to be praised than outstanding talent. Most talents are to some extent a gift. Good character, by contrast, is not given to us. We have to build it piece by piece by thought, choice, courage and determination."

John Luther

"I admire men of character, and I judge character not by how men deal with their superiors, but mostly how they deal with their subordinates, and that, to me, is where you find out what the character of a man is."

General H. Norman Schwartzkopf (1934 -), American army officer.

"I care not what others think of what I do, but I care very much about what I of what I do. That is character!"

Theodore Roosevelt (1858 - 1919), 26th US President (1901 - 1909).

"I have a dream that my four little children will one day live in a nation where they will not be judged by the color of their skin but by the content of their character."

Martin Luther King Jr. (1929 - 1968), American civil rights leader and Nobel Peace Prize winner.

"I hope I shall possess firmness and virtue enough to maintain what I consider the most enviable of all titles, the character of an honest man."

George Washington (1732 - 1799), 1st US President (1789 - 1797) and a military leader during the American Revolution.

"If you don't stand for something, you'll fall for anything."

Peter Marshall

"If you tell the truth you don't have to remember anything."

Mark Twain, the pen name of Samuel Langhorne Clemens (1835 – 1910), American writer and humorist.

"Life is a series of experiences, each of which makes us bigger, even though it is hard to realize this. For the world was built to develop character, and we must learn that the setbacks and grieves which we endure help us in our marching onward."

Henry Ford (1863 - 1947), prominent American industrialist, the founder of the Ford Motor Company, and sponsor of the development of the assembly line technique of mass production.

"Most people say that is it is the intellect which makes a great scientist. They are wrong: it is character."

Albert Einstein (1879 - 1955), German-born American physicist who developed the theories of relativity and won the Nobel Prize for Physics in 1921.

"Nothing shows a man's character more than what he laughs at."

Johann Wolfgang von Goethe (1749 - 1832), German writer, philosopher and scientist.

"Our character is shaped as much by our failures as it is by our successes."

John Gray

"Out of our beliefs are born deeds; out of our deeds we form habits; out of our habits grows our character; and on our character we build our destiny."

Henry Hancock (1822 - 1883), Harvard-trained American lawyer and a land surveyor working in California in the 1850s. He was the owner of Rancho La Brea, which included the La Brea Tar Pits.

"Parents can only give good advice or put them on the right paths, but the final forming of a person's character lies in their own hands."

Anne Frank (1929 - 1945), one of the most renowned and most discussed Jewish victims of the Holocaust. Acknowledged for the quality of her writing, her diary has become one of the world's most widely read books, and has been the basis for several plays and films.

"People do not seem to realize that their opinion of the world is also a confession of character."

Ralph Waldo Emerson (1803 - 1882), American writer and poet.

"People grow through experience if they meet life honestly and courageously. This is how character is built."

Eleanor Roosevelt (1884 - 1962), 32nd US first lady (1933 - 1945), UN diplomat and humanitarian.

"Take care of your character and your reputation will take care of itself."

Unknown

"The collapse of character begins with compromise."

Unknown

"The foundation stones for a balanced success are honesty, character, integrity, faith, love and loyalty."

Zig Ziglar (1926 -), American author, salesman, and motivational speaker.

"The true measure of a man is how he treats someone who can do him absolutely no good."

Samuel Johnson (1709 - 1784), English author who made lasting contributions to English literature as a poet, essayist, moralist, literary critic, biographer, editor and lexicographer.

"The true test of character is not how much we know how to do, but how we behave when we don't know what to do."

John W. Holt Jr.

"The ultimate measure of a man is not where he stands in moments of comfort and convenience, but where he stands at times of challenge and controversy."

Martin Luther King Jr. (1929 - 1968), American civil rights leader and Nobel Peace Prize winner.

"Thoughts lead on to purpose, purpose leads on to actions, actions form habits, habits decide character, and character fixes our destiny."

Tryon Edwards (1809 - 1894), American theologian.

"Try not to become a man of success, but rather try to become a man of value."

Albert Einstein (1879 - 1955), German-born American physicist who developed the theories of relativity and won the Nobel Prize for Physics in 1921.

"Watch your thoughts, for they become words. Watch your words, for they become actions. Watch your actions, for they become habits. Watch your habits, for they become character. Watch your character, for it becomes your destiny."

Heraclitus of Ephesus (~ 535 BC - 475 BC), a pre-Socratic Greek philosopher.

"You cannot build character and courage by taking away man's initiative and independence."

Abraham Lincoln (1809 - 1865), 16th US President. His term of office was from 1861 to 1865 and included the American Civil War.

"You cannot dream yourself into a character; you must hammer and forge yourself one."

James A. Froude (1818 - 1894), English historian, novelist, biographer and editor.

"You will make a lousy anybody else, but you are the best you in existence."

Zig Ziglar (1926 -), American author, salesman, and motivational speaker.

children family
grandparents hate love mistakes mother older
parenting praise roots teenagers wings

"A child will perform from their mind for their coach/teacher, but for a parent they perform from their heart."

Unknown

"A mother holds her children's hands for a while, their hearts forever."

Unknown

"And it is time for those who talk about family values to start valuing families."

Senator John Kerry (1943 -), American Senator.

"Be nice to your kids. They'll choose your nursing home."

Unknown

"Before I got married I had six theories about bringing up children; now I have six children, and no theories."

John Wilmont

"Children are the world's most valuable resource and its best hope for the future."

John F. Kennedy (1917 - 1963), 35th US President (1961 - 1963).

"Children need love the most when they deserve it the least."

Erma Bombeck (1927 - 1996), American humorist who achieved great popularity for her newspaper column that described suburban home life from the mid-1960s until the late 1990s. Bombeck also published 15 books, most of which became best-sellers.

"Children need your presence much more than your presents."

Jesse Jackson (1941 -), American civil rights activist and Baptist minister.

"Children seldom misquote you. In fact, they usually repeat word for word what you shouldn't have said."

Unknown

"Children will not remember you for the material things you provided but for the feeling that you cherished them."

Richard L. Evans (1906 - 1971), American, was a member of the Quorum of the Twelve Apostles of The Church of Jesus Christ of Latter-day Saints (1953 - 1971), the president of Rotary International (1966 - 1967), and the writer, producer, and announcer of *Music and the Spoken Word* for forty-one years (1929–1971).

"Don't worry that children never listen to you; worry that they are always watching you."

Robert Fulghum (1937 -), American author, painter, sculptor and former minister.

"Getting older, everything gets worse; except forgetfulness... that gets better."

Unknown

"Grandparents: the people who think your children are wonderful even though they're sure you're not raising them right."

Unknown

"Having one child makes you a parent; having two makes you are a referee."

David Frost (1939 -), British journalist, comedian, writer and media personality, best known for his serious interviews with various political figures, the most notable being Richard Nixon.

"In every conceivable manner, the family is link to our past, bridge to our future."

Alex Haley (1921 - 1992), African-American writer best known as the author of "Roots: The Saga of an American Family" and the co-author of "The Autobiography of Malcolm X."

"If you have never been hated by your child, you have never been a parent."

Bette Davis (1908 - 1989), American actress of film, television and theater.

"It is a wise child that knows its own father, and an unusual one that unreservedly approves of him."

Mark Twain, the pen name of Samuel Langhorne Clemens (1835 – 1910), American writer and humorist.

"It is not what a teenager knows that worries his parents. It's how he found out."

Unknown

"Let us put our minds together and see what life we can make for our children."

Sitting Bull (1831 - 1890), Hunkpapa Lakota Sioux holy man who led his people as a tribal chief during years of resistance to US government policies.

"Mistakes are a natural part of growing up. They're to be expected and made light of. But children bloom like spring flowers under praise. They want so much to be noticed and appreciated, to excel and have that excellence noticed."

Earl Nightingale (1921 - 1989), American motivational speaker and author, known as the "Dean of Personal Development."

"My wife has been my closest friend, my closest advisor. And ... she's not somebody who looks to the limelight, or even is wild about me being in politics. And that's a good reality check on me. When I go home, she wants me to be a good father and a good husband. And everything else is secondary to that."

President Barack H. Obama (1961 -), American, 44th US President and first African-American President.

"Never underestimate a parent's ability to mortify his child."

Peter Gallagher (1955 -), American actor, musician and writer.

"Our greatest natural resource is the minds of our children."

Walt Disney (1901 - 1966), American film producer, director, screenwriter, voice actor, animator, entrepreneur, entertainer, international icon, and philanthropist. Disney is famous for his influence in the field of entertainment during the 20th century. As the Co-Founder (with his brother Roy O. Disney) of Walt Disney Productions, Disney became one of the best-known motion picture producers in the world. The corporation he co-founded, now known as The Walt Disney Company, today has annual revenues of approximately $35 billion.

"Parents are so excited about the first steps and words of their children, but then they spend the next 17 years telling them to sit down and shut up."

Unknown

"Parents often talk about the younger generation as if they didn't have anything to do with it."

Haim Ginott (1922 - 1973), teacher, child psychologist and psychotherapist who worked with children and parents.

"Parents should work hard to give their children everything money cannot buy."

Unknown

"Setting a good example for your children takes all the fun out of middle age."

William Feather (1889 - 1981), American publisher and author. From "The Business of Life" (1949).

"The best thing you can spend on your children is time."

Unknown

"The greatest gifts you can give your children are the roots of responsibility and the wings of independence."

Denis Waitley (1933 -), American motivational speaker and writer, consultant and best-selling author.

"There are times when parenthood seems nothing more than feeding the hand that bites you."

Peter De Vries (1910 - 1993), American comic visionary, editor, novelist, satirist and linguist.

"There are two lasting bequests we can give our children. One is roots, the other is wings."

Hodding Carter, Jr. (1907 - 1972), prominent Southern US progressive journalist and author.

"There is no friendship, no love, like that of the parent for the child."

Henry Ward Beecher (1813 - 1887), prominent American Congregationalist clergyman, social reformer, abolitionist, and speaker in the mid to late 19th century.

"What a bargain grandchildren are! I give them my loose change, and they give me a million dollars' worth of pleasure."

Gene Perret

"What feeling is so nice as a child's hand in yours? So small, so soft and warm, like a kitten huddling in the shelter of your clasp."

Marjorie Holmes

"While we try to teach our children all about life, our children teach us what life is all about."

Angela Schwindt

"You know your children are growing up when they stop asking you where they came from and refuse to tell you where they're going."

P.J. O'Rourke (1947 -), American political satirist, journalist, writer, and author.

enemies
compassion dreams earth   footprints
friends
future guest heart helping house money
mortal others

"A friend is one that knows you as you are, understands where you have been, accepts what you have become, and still, gently allows you to grow."

William Shakespeare (1564 - 1616), one of England's greatest playwrights.

"A friend is someone that won't begin to talk behind your back when you leave the room."

Unknown

"A friend is someone who knows the song in your heart and sings it back to you when you have forgotten how it goes."

Unknown

"A friend is someone who understands your past, believes in your future, and accepts you just the way you are."

Unknown

"A perfect guest is one who makes his host feel at home."

Unknown

"A true friend is someone who thinks that you are a good egg even though he knows that you are slightly cracked."

Bernard C. Meltzer (1916 - 1998), American radio host best known for his advice call-in show, "What's Your Problem?"

"Be slow in choosing a friend, slower in changing."

Benjamin Franklin (1706 - 1790), American statesman, scientist, writer and printer.

"Few things can help an individual more than to place responsibility on him and to let him know that you trust him."

Booker T. Washington (1856 - 1915), American educator and political activist.

"Friends are the family we choose for ourselves."

Edna Buchanan (1939 -), American journalist and author best known for her crime mystery novels.

"Friends . . . They cherish one another's hopes. They are kind to one another's dreams."

Henry David Thoreau (1817 - 1862), American writer, poet and philosopher.

"Friendship is a living thing that lasts only as long as it is nourished with kindness, empathy and understanding."

Unknown

"Friendship is a strong and habitual inclination in two persons to promote the good and happiness of one another."

Eustace Budgell (1686 - 1737), English writer and politician.

"Friendship is like money, easier made than kept."

Samuel Butler

"Here's to good friends, who know you well, and like you anyway!"

Toast (Unknown)

"He's my friend that speaks well of me behind my back."

Thomas Fuller (1608 - 1661), British clergyman and writer.

"If you are looking for friends when you need them, it's too late."

Mark Twain, the pen name of Samuel Langhorne Clemens (1835 – 1910), American writer and humorist.

"It was a friendship founded on business, which is a good deal better than a business founded on friendship."

John D. Rockefeller (1839 - 1937), American oil magnate who revolutionized the petroleum industry and defined the structure of modern philanthropy.

"Keep your friends close and your enemies closer."

"Michael Corleone" in the movie "The Godfather, Part II."

"Life is partly what we make it, and partly what it is made by the friends we choose."

Tennessee Williams (1911 - 1983), American playwright.

"Life is to be fortified by many friendships. To love and to be loved is the greatest happiness of existence."

Sydney Smith (1771 - 1845), English clergyman, essayist and wit.

"Many people will walk in and out of your life, but only true friends will leave footprints in your heart."

Eleanor Roosevelt (1884 - 1962), 32nd US first lady (1933 - 1945), UN diplomat and humanitarian.

"New friends are silver, old friends are gold. Always make new friends, but don't forget the old."

Joseph Parry (1841 - 1903), Welsh composer and musician.

"Nobody will ever win the battle of the sexes. There's too much fraternizing with the enemy."

Henry Kissinger (1923 -), German-born American political scientist, diplomat, and recipient of the Nobel Peace Prize. He served as National Security Advisor and later concurrently as Secretary of State in the administrations of Presidents Richard Nixon and Gerald Ford. After his term, his opinion was still sought by many following presidents and many world leaders.

"Sometimes the best helping hand you can give is a good, firm push."

Unknown

"The bank of friendship cannot exist for long without deposits."

Unknown

"The most beautiful discovery two friends can make is that they can grow separately without growing apart."

Unknown

"The only really decent thing to do behind a person's back is pat it."

Unknown

"True friendship comes when the silence between two people is comfortable."

David Tyson Gentry

"What we have done for ourselves alone dies with us; what we have done for others and the world remains and is immortal."

Albert Pike

"You have enemies? Good. That means you've stood up for something, sometime in your life."

Sir Winston Churchill (1874 - 1965), British orator, author and Prime Minister during World War II.

aid americans committees congress corruption crimes criminals debts
democracy education fairness firm fool foreign
government
healthcare idiot law liberal
politics
majority man newspapers subsidies tax
taxidermist voters war winners

"A government big enough to give you everything you want, is strong enough to take everything you have."

Thomas Jefferson (1743 - 1826), 3rd US President (1801 - 1809) and the primary writer of the Declaration of Independence in 1776.

"A government which robs Peter to pay Paul can always depend on the support of Paul."

George Bernard Shaw (1856 - 1950), Irish writer and playwright who won the 1925 Nobel Prize for Literature.

"A liberal is someone who feels a great debt to his fellow man, which debt he proposes to pay off with your money."

G. Gordon Liddy (1930 -), American. Was an organizer and director of the burglaries of the Democratic National Committee headquarters in the Watergate building in May and June of 1972.

"A typical vice of American politics is the avoidance of saying anything real on real issues."

Theodore Roosevelt (1858 - 1919), 26th US President (1901 - 1909), from a speech in New York, September 7, 1903.

"An honest politician is one who, when he is bought, will stay bought."

Simon Cameron (1799 - 1889), American politician who, after making his fortune in railways and banking, turned to a life of politics. He served as US Secretary of War for Abraham Lincoln at the start of the American Civil War.

"Democracy is being allowed to vote for the candidate you dislike least."

Robert Byrne (1930 -), American author and champion billiards player.

"Democracy must be something more than two wolves and a sheep voting on what to have for dinner."

James Bovard (1956 -), American libertarian author and lecturer, and model whose political commentary targets examples of waste, failures, corruption, cronyism and abuses of power in government.

"Foreign aid might be defined as a transfer of money from poor people in rich countries to rich people in poor countries."

Douglas Casey, American free market economist, best-selling financial author, and international investor and entrepreneur.

"Giving money and power to government is like giving whiskey and car keys to teenage boys."

P.J. O'Rourke (1947 -), American political satirist, journalist, writer, and author.

"Government is not reason, it is not eloquence, it is force; like fire, a troublesome servant and a fearful master. Never for a moment should it be left to irresponsible action."

George Washington (1732 - 1799), 1st US President (1789 - 1797) and a military leader during the American Revolution.

"Government is the great fiction, through which everybody endeavors to live at the expense of everybody else."

Frederic Bastiat (1801 - 1850), French economist.

"Government's view of the economy could be summed up in a few short phrases: if it moves, tax it. If it keeps moving, regulate it. And if it stops moving, subsidize it."

Ronald Reagan (1911 - 2004), actor, 33rd Governor of California (1967 - 1975) and 40th US President (1981 - 1989). From a 1986 speech.

"I contend that for a nation to try to tax itself into prosperity is like a man standing in a bucket and trying to lift himself up by the handle."

Sir Winston Churchill (1874 - 1965), British orator, author and Prime Minister during World War II.

"I don't make jokes. I just watch the government and report the facts."

Will Rogers (1879 -1935) Cherokee-American cowboy, social commentator.

"I have been thinking that I would make a proposition to my Republican friends... that if they will stop telling lies about the Democrats, we will stop telling the truth about them."

Adlai E. Stevenson (1900-1965), American politician who was Governor of Illinois (1949 - 1953) and Ambassador to the United Nations (1961 - 1965).

"I have come to the conclusion that one useless man is a disgrace, two are called a law firm and three or more become a congress."

John Adams (1735 - 1826), 2nd US President (1797 - 1801), in his frustration with the Continental Congress.

"I like to believe that people in the long run are going to do more to promote peace than our governments. Indeed, I think that people want peace so much that one of these days governments had better get out of the way and let them have it."

Dwight D. Eisenhower, General and 34th US President (1953 - 1961).

"If you don't read the newspaper you are uninformed, if you do read the newspaper you are misinformed."

Mark Twain, the pen name of Samuel Langhorne Clemens (1835 – 1910), American writer and humorist.

"If you think healthcare is expensive now, wait until you see what it costs when it's free!"

P.J. O'Rourke (1947 -), American political satirist, journalist, writer, and author.

"If you want to kill any idea in the world, get a committee working on it."

Charles F. Kettering (1876 - 1958), American inventor, engineer, businessman, and the holder of 140 patents.

"In general, the art of government consists of taking as much money as possible from one party of the citizens to give to the other."

Voltaire (1694 - 1778), French writer and philosopher.

"It has been said that democracy is the worst form of government except all the others that have been tried."

Sir Winston Churchill (1874 - 1965), British orator, author and Prime Minister during World War II.

"It'll be a great day when education gets all the money it wants and the Air Force has to hold a bake sale to buy bombers."

Robert Fulghum (1937 -), American author, painter, sculptor and former minister.

"Just because you do not take an interest in politics doesn't mean politics won't take an interest in you!"

Pericles (495 BC - 429 BC), prominent and influential Greek statesman, orator, and general of Athens.

"Many a man goes into politics with a fine future and comes out with a terrible past."

Unknown

"My experience in government is that when things are non-controversial and beautifully coordinated, there is not much going on."

John F. Kennedy (1917 - 1963), 35th US President (1961 - 1963).

"Ninety percent of the politicians give the other ten percent a bad reputation."

Henry Kissinger (1923 -), German-born American political scientist, diplomat, and recipient of the Nobel Peace Prize. He served as National Security Advisor and later concurrently as Secretary of State in the administrations of Presidents Richard Nixon and Gerald Ford. After his term, his opinion was still sought by many following presidents and many world leaders.

"No man's life, liberty, or property is safe while the legislature is in session."

Mark Twain, the pen name of Samuel Langhorne Clemens (1835 – 1910), American writer and humorist.

"One of the penalties for refusing to participate in politics is that you end up being governed by your inferiors."

Plato (~ 427 BC - 347 BC), Ancient Greek writer and philosopher and a student of Socrates. Plato's most famous student was Aristotle.

"Only the winners decide what were war crimes."

Garry Wills (1934 -), American Pulitzer Prize-winning and prolific author, journalist, and historian, specializing in American politics, American political history and ideology and the Roman Catholic Church.

"Patriotism is often an arbitrary veneration of real estate above principles."

George Jean Nathan (1882 - 1958), American drama critic and editor.

"Politics: 'Poli' a Latin word meaning 'many'; and 'tics' meaning 'bloodsucking creatures'."

Robin Williams (1951 -), American actor and comedian. Rising to fame with his role as the alien Mork in the TV series *Mork and Mindy*, and later stand-up comedy work, Williams has performed in many feature films since 1980. He won the Academy Award for Best Supporting Actor for his performance in the 1997 film "Good Will Hunting."

"Sometimes the majority only means that all the fools are on the same side."

Unknown

"Suppose you were an idiot and suppose you were a member of Congress. But I repeat myself."

Mark Twain, the pen name of Samuel Langhorne Clemens (1835 – 1910), American writer and humorist.

"Talk is cheap...except when Congress does it."

Cullen Hightower (1923 -), well known American quotation and quip writer often associated with the conservative political movement.

"The best argument against democracy is a five-minute conversation with the average voter."

Sir Winston Churchill (1874 - 1965), British orator, author and Prime Minister during World War II.

"The Constitution is not an instrument for the government to restrain the people, it is an instrument for the people to restrain the government - lest it come to dominate our lives and interests."

Patrick Henry (1736 - 1799), American orator and politician who led the movement for independence in Virginia in the 1770s. A Founding Father, he served as the first and sixth post-colonial Governor of Virginia from 1776 to 1779 and subsequently, from 1784 to 1786. Henry led the opposition to the Stamp Act of 1765 and is well remembered for his "Give me Liberty, or give me Death!" speech.

"The government is like a baby's alimentary canal, with a happy appetite at one end and no responsibility at the other."

Ronald Reagan (1911 - 2004), actor, 33rd Governor of California (1967 - 1975) and 40th US President (1981 - 1989).

"The government of the United States is not in any sense founded on the Christian Religion."

George Washington (1732 - 1799), 1st US President (1789 - 1797) and a military leader during the American Revolution.

"The introduction of religious passion into politics is the end of honest politics, and the introduction of politics into religion is the prostitution of true religion."

Lord Hailsham (1872 - 1950), British lawyer and politician.

"The only difference between a tax man and a taxidermist is that the taxidermist leaves the skin."

Mark Twain, the pen name of Samuel Langhorne Clemens (1835 – 1910), American writer and humorist.

"There is no distinctly native American criminal class...save Congress."

Mark Twain, the pen name of Samuel Langhorne Clemens (1835 – 1910), American writer and humorist.

"There is no monument dedicated to the memory of a committee."

Lester J. Pourciau

"There's no trick to being a humorist when you have the whole government working for you."

Will Rogers (1879 -1935) Cherokee-American cowboy, social commentator.

"They want the federal government controlling Social Security like it's some kind of federal program."

George W. Bush (1946 -), 43rd President of the US (2001 - 2009) and 46th Governor of Texas (1995 - 2000).

"What experience and history teaches us is that people and governments have never learned anything from history, or acted on principles deduced from it."

Georg Wilhelm Friedrich Hegel (1770 - 1831), German philosopher and inventor.

"What this country needs are more unemployed politicians."

Edward Langley (1928 - 1995), artist.

"When I am abroad, I always make it a rule to never criticize or attack the government of my own country. I make up for lost time when I come home."

Sir Winston Churchill (1874 - 1965), British orator, author and Prime Minister during World War II.

"When they call the roll in the Senate, the Senators do not know whether to answer 'Present' or 'Not guilty.'"

Theodore Roosevelt (1858 - 1919), 26th US President (1901 - 1909).

"Why does the Air Force need expensive new bombers? Have the people we've been bombing over the years been complaining?"

George Wallace (1919 - 1998), American Governor of Alabama.

"You can always count on the American people to do the right thing. Once they have exhausted all of the alternatives."

Sir Winston Churchill (1874 - 1965), British orator, author and Prime Minister during World War II.

happiness

bliss contentment control dreams enjoyment excellence future ignorance imperfections love past present satisfaction worrying

"A happy person is not a person in a certain set of circumstances, but rather a person with a certain set of attitudes."

Hugh Downs (1921 -), retired American broadcaster, television host, producer, and author. He served as anchor of *20/20*, host of *The Today Show*, announcer for *The Tonight Show with Jack Paar*, host of the *Concentration* game show, host of the PBS talk show *Over Easy* and co-host of the syndicated talk show *Not for Women Only*.

"Anything you're good at contributes to happiness."

Bertrand Russell (1872 - 1970), English logician and philosopher.

"Being happy doesn't mean that everything is perfect. It means that you've decided to look beyond the imperfections."

Unknown

"Don't wish me happiness - I don't expect to be happy It's gotten beyond that, somehow. Wish me courage and strength and a sense of humor - I will need them all."

Anne Morrow Lindbergh (1906 - 2001), a pioneering American aviator, author, and the spouse of fellow aviator Charles Lindbergh.

"Happiness comes of the capacity to feel deeply, to enjoy simply, to think freely, to risk life, to be needed."

Storm Jameson (1891 - 1986), English writer, known for her 45 novels, and criticism.

"Happiness is a butterfly, which when pursued, is always just beyond your grasp, but which, if you will sit down quietly, may alight upon you."

Nathaniel Hawthorne (1804 - 1864), American novelist and short story writer best known for *The Scarlet Letter* (published in 1850).

"Happiness is a path, not a destination."

Unknown

"Happiness is an attitude. We either make ourselves miserable, or happy and strong. The amount of work is the same."

Francesca Reigler

"Happiness is inward and not outward; and so it does not depend on what we have, but on what we are."

Henry Van Dyke (1852 - 1933), American short-story writer, poet and essayist.

"Happiness is like a kiss...you must share it to enjoy it."

Bernard Meltzer (1916 - 1998), American radio host for several decades. His advice call-in show, "What's Your Problem?," aired from 1967 until the mid-1990s.

"Happiness is not something you have in your hands; it is something you carry in your heart."

Unknown

"Happiness is the meaning and the purpose of life, the whole aim and end of human existence."

Aristotle (384 - 322 BC), Greek writer, teacher and philosopher, often considered the father of logic.

"Happiness isn't having what you want, it's wanting what you have."

Unknown

"Happiness? That's nothing more than a good health and a poor memory."

Albert Schweitzer (1875 - 1965), Franco-German (Alsatian) theologian, organist, philosopher, physician, and medical missionary.

"Happy are those who dream dreams and are ready to pay the price to make them come true."

Leon Joseph Suenens (1904 - 1996), Belgian Archbishop and Cardinal of the Roman Catholic Church.

"I, not events, have the power to make me happy or unhappy today. I can choose which it shall be. Yesterday is dead, tomorrow hasn't arrived yet. I have just one day, today, and I'm going to be happy in it."

Groucho Marx (1890 - 1977), American comedian and film star famed as a master of wit.

"If ignorance is bliss, why aren't more people happy?"

Thomas Jefferson (1743 - 1826), 3rd US President (1801 - 1809) and the primary writer of the Declaration of Independence in 1776.

"It is not how much we have, but how much we enjoy, that makes happiness."

Charles H. Spurgeon (1834 - 1892), English writer and clergyman.

"It isn't what you have, or who you are, or where you are, or what you are doing that makes you happy or unhappy. It is what you think about."

Dale Carnegie (1888 - 1955), American writer, lecturer, and the developer of famous courses in self-improvement, salesmanship, corporate training, public speaking, and interpersonal skills. He's best known as author of "How to Win Friends and Influence People" (1936).

"Most people are about as happy as they make up their minds to be."

Abraham Lincoln (1809 - 1865), 16th US President. His term of office was from 1861 to 1865 and included the American Civil War.

"Now and then it's good to pause in our pursuit of happiness and just be happy."

Guillaume Apollinaire (1880 - 1918), French poet and critic.

"People would enjoy life more if, once they got what they wanted, they could remember how much they wanted it."

Unknown

"Some people bring happiness wherever they go, others whenever they go."

Oscar Wilde (1854 - 1900), Irish dramatist, novelist and poet.

"Some pursue happiness - others create it."

Unknown

"The ancient Greek definition of happiness was the full use of your powers along lines of excellence."

John F. Kennedy (1917 - 1963), 35th US President (1961 - 1963).

"The best way to cheer yourself up is to try to cheer somebody else up."

Mark Twain, the pen name of Samuel Langhorne Clemens (1835 – 1910), American writer and humorist.

"The greatest happiness of life is the conviction that we are loved - loved for ourselves, or rather, loved in spite of ourselves."

Victor Hugo (1802 - 1885), French writer and poet.

"The greatest happiness is to transform one's feelings into action."

Madame de Staël (1766 - 1817), French-speaking Swiss author living in Paris and abroad who influenced literary tastes in Europe at the turn of the 19th century.

"The pursuit of happiness is a most ridiculous phrase; if you pursue happiness you'll never find it."

C.P. Snow (1905 - 1980), English physicist and novelist who also served in several important positions with the UK government.

"The reason people find it so hard to be happy is that they always see the past better than it was, the present worse than it is, and the future less resolved than it will be."

Marcel Pagnol (1895 - 1974), French writer, producer and film director.

"There is only one happiness in this life, to love and be loved."

George Sands (1804 - 1876), French romantic writer.

"There is only one way to happiness and that is to cease worrying about things which are beyond the power of our will."

Epictetus (55 AD - 135 AD), Greek Stoic philosopher.

"To be kind to all, to like many and love a few, to be needed and wanted by those we love, is certainly the nearest we can come to happiness."

Mary Stuart (1542 - 1587), Scottish Queen.

"To find your own way is to follow your bliss. This involves analysis, watching yourself and seeing where real deep bliss is -- not the quick little excitement, but the real deep, life-filling bliss."

Joseph Campbell (1904 - 1987), prolific American author, editor, philosopher and teacher.

"To me, there are three things we all should do every day. We should do this every day of our lives. Number one is laugh. You should laugh every day. Number two is think. You should spend some time in thought. And number three is, you should have your emotions moved to tears, could be happiness or joy. But think about it. If you laugh, you think, and you cry, that's a full day. That's a heck of a day. You do that seven days a week, you're going to have something special."

Jim Valvano (1946 - 1993), American college basketball coach. While the head coach at North Carolina State University, he won the 1983 NCAA Basketball Tournament against high odds. Valvano is not only remembered for running up and down the court after winning the 1983 NCAA championship, seemingly in disbelief and looking for someone to hug, but also for his inspirational 1993 ESPY Awards speech, given just eight weeks before he died of cancer.

"True happiness may be sought, thought, or caught -- but never bought."

Unknown

"We act as though comfort and luxury were the chief requirements of life, when all that we need to make us really happy is something to be enthusiastic about."

Charles Kingsley (1819 - 1875), British Anglican clergyman, teacher and writer whose novels, widely read in the Victorian era, influenced social developments in Britain.

"We tend to forget that happiness doesn't come as a result of getting something we don't have, but rather of recognizing and appreciating what we do have."

Frederick Keonig

"You can easily find people who are ten times as rich at sixty as they were at twenty; but not one of them will tell you that they are ten times as happy."

George Bernard Shaw (1856 - 1950), Irish writer and playwright who won the 1925 Nobel Prize for Literature.

accidents aging **animals** attitude binary **cats** contemplation criticism decisions diet **dogs** drinking dyslexia excess face fight food french future gravity hockey hollywood **humor** impromptu language life mistakes moderation obituaries parenting perfect personal growth **pigs** pirate **predictions** pregnancy principles proofreading psychokinesis restaurants safari speech spelling sports **statistics** success temptation water wine wrestling

"43% of all statistics are worthless."

Unknown

"7/5th of all people do not understand fractions."

Unknown

"90% of success is just showing up."

Woody Allen (1935 -), American screenwriter, director, actor, comedian, jazz musician, author, and playwright. Allen's distinctive films, which run the gamut from dramas to screwball sex comedies, have made him a notable American director.

"95% of all statistics are false."

Unknown

"A day for firm decisions! Or is it?"

Unknown

"A day without sunshine is like night."

Unknown

"A dog thinks: Hey, these people I live with feed me, love me, provide me with a nice warm, dry house, pet me, and take good care of me... They must be Gods! A cat thinks: Hey, these people I live with feed me, love me, provide me with a nice warm, dry house, pet me, and take good care of me... I must be a God!"

Unknown

"Adults are always asking little kids what they want to be when they grow up because they're looking for ideas."

Paula Poundstone (1959 -), American comic.

"All those who believe in psychokinesis raise my hand."

Steven Wright (1955 -), American comedian, actor and writer.

"Bad spellers of the world untie!"

Unknown

"Be alert – the world needs more lerts."

Unknown

"Be safety conscious. 80% of people are caused by accidents."

Unknown

"Before you criticize someone, walk a mile in their shoes. That way, if he gets angry, he's a mile away and barefoot."

Unknown

"Change is inevitable, except from vending machines."

Robert C. Gallagher

"Don't sweat the petty things and don't pet the sweaty things."

George Carlin (1937 - 2008), American stand-up comedian, social critic, actor and author, who won five Grammy Awards for his comedy albums.

"Duct tape is like the force; it has a light side and a dark side and it holds the universe together."

Oprah Winfrey (1954 -), American television host, actress, producer, and philanthropist, best known for her self-titled, multi-award winning talk show, which has become the highest-rated program of its kind in history. She has been ranked the richest African American of the 20th century, the greatest black philanthropist in American history, and was once the world's only black billionaire. She is also, according to some assessments, the most influential woman in the world.

"Dyslexics have more fnu."

Unknown

"Entropy isn't what it used to be."

Unknown

"Every time I find the meaning of life, they change it."

Unknown

"Excess on occasion is exhilarating. It prevents moderation from acquiring the deadening effect of a habit."

W. Somerset Maugham (1874 - 1965), English playwright, novelist and short story writer. He was among the most popular writers of his era and, reputedly, the highest paid author during the 1930s.

"Gravity. . . Not just a good idea: it's the law."

Unknown

"Half this game is 90% mental."

Yogi Berra (1925 -), former American Major League Baseball player and manager. He played almost his entire 19-year baseball career (1946 - 1965) for the New York Yankees.

"Hollywood is a place where people from Iowa mistake each other for stars."

Fred Allen (1894 - 1956), American comedian and radio show host.

"Humor helps us to think out of the box. The average child laughs about 400 times per day, the average adult laughs only 15 times per day. What happened to the other 385 laughs?"

Unknown

"I don't have any solution, but I certainly admire the problem."

Ashleigh Brilliant (1933 -), British-born American author and syndicated cartoonist.

"I generally avoid temptation unless I can't resist it."

Mae West (1893 - 1980), American actress, playwright, screenwriter and sex symbol.

"I get up in the morning and read the obituary column. If I'm not in it I have breakfast."

Unknown

"I like pigs better than cat and dogs. Dogs are subservient and look up to man. Cats are aloof and look down on man. A pig, however, will look you in the eye, and see his equal."

Sir Winston Churchill (1874 - 1965), British orator, author and Prime Minister during World War II.

"I never forget a face, but in your case I'll be glad to make an exception."

Groucho Marx (1890 - 1977), American comedian and film star famed as a master of wit.

"I spent 90% of my money on women, drink and fast cars. The rest I wasted."

George Best (1946 - 2005), Irish professional football player, best known for his years with Manchester United.

"I still miss my ex. But my aim is getting better."

Unknown

"I take my children everywhere, but they always find their way back home."

Robert Orben (1927 -), American magician, professional comedy writer and author of books for magicians. He wrote a book called "Speaker's Handbook of Humor".

"I was lying in bed one evening, looking up at the starlit sky above...gazing through the deep blue abyss, I thought to myself: "where the heck is my roof?"

Unknown

"I was standing in the park wondering why frisbees got bigger as they closer. Then it hit me."

Unknown

"I went on a diet, swore off drinking and heavy eating, and in fourteen days I lost two weeks."

Joe E. Lewis (1902 - 1971), American comedian and singer.

"I went to a fight and a hockey game broke out."

Rodney Dangerfield (1921 - 2004), American comedian and actor.

"I'd rather have a bottle in front of me than a frontal lobotomy."

Dorothy Parker (1893 - 1967), American short-story writer and poet.

"If someone had told me I would be Pope one day, I would have studied harder."

Pope John Paul I (1912 - 1978), Italian Pope.

"I'm a nobody, nobody is perfect, therefore I'm perfect."

Unknown

"In life one often experiences Deja Moo -- the feeling you've heard this bull before."

Unknown

"In Paris they simply stared when I spoke to them in French; I never did succeed in making those idiots understand their own language."

Mark Twain, the pen name of Samuel Langhorne Clemens (1835 – 1910), American writer and humorist.

"Is ignorance or apathy the biggest problem with the world today? I don't know and I don't care."

Unknown

"It usually takes more than three weeks to prepare a good impromptu speech."

Mark Twain, the pen name of Samuel Langhorne Clemens (1835 – 1910), American writer and humorist.

"It's déjà vu ... all over again!"

Yogi Berra (1925 -), former American Major League Baseball player and manager. He played almost his entire 19-year baseball career (1946 - 1965) for the New York Yankees.

"It's hard for me to get used to these changing times. I can remember when the air was clean and sex was dirty."

George Burns (1896 - 1996), American comedian, actor, and writer.

"Never eat yellow snow."

Unknown

"Never try to impress a woman, because if you do she'll expect you to keep up the standard for the rest of your life."

W.C. Fields (1880 - 1946), American comedian, actor, juggler and writer. Fields was known for his comic persona as a misanthropic and hard-drinking egotist who remained a sympathetic character despite his snarling contempt for dogs, children, and women.

"Never wrestle with a pig. You both get all dirty, and the pig likes it."

Unknown

"Never, ever make absolute, unconditional statements."

Unknown

"Nobody goes to that restaurant anymore. It's too crowded."

Yogi Berra (1925 -), former American Major League Baseball player and manager. He played almost his entire 19-year baseball career (1946 - 1965) for the New York Yankees.

"Oh, you hate your job? Why didn't you say so? There's a support group for that. It's called EVERYBODY, and they meet at the bar. "

Drew Carey (1958 -), American comedian.

"Once I thought I was wrong, but I was mistaken."

Unknown

"Proofread carefully to see if you any words out."

Dave Barry (1947 -), Pulitzer Prize-winning American author and columnist, who wrote a nationally syndicated humor column for The Miami Herald from 1983 to 2005. He has also written numerous books of humor and parody, as well as comedic novels.

"Reminds me of my safari in Africa. Somebody forgot the corkscrew and for several days we had to live on nothing but food and water."

W.C. Fields (1880 - 1946), American comedian, actor, juggler and writer. Fields was known for his comic persona as a misanthropic and hard-drinking egotist who remained a sympathetic character despite his snarling contempt for dogs, children, and women.

"Sometimes I lie awake at night, and ask, 'Where have I gone wrong?' Then a voice says to me, 'This is going to take more than one night.'"

Charles Schulz (1922 - 2000), American cartoonist best known for his comic strip "Peanuts."

"Some people can tell what time it is by looking at the sun, but I never have been able to make out the numbers."

Unknown

"Spelling is a lossed art."

Unknown

"The hard thing about making predictions is the future."

Yogi Berra (1925 -), former American Major League Baseball player and manager. He played almost his entire 19-year baseball career (1946 - 1965) for the New York Yankees.

"There are 10 kinds of people in the world: those who understand binary, and those who don't."

Unknown

"There are three types of people - those who can count and those who can't."

Unknown

"These are my principles - if you don't like them, I have others."

Groucho Marx (1890 - 1977), American comedian and film star famed as a master of wit.

"Time flies like an arrow. Fruit flies like a banana."

Groucho Marx (1890 - 1977), American comedian and film star famed as a master of wit.

"To err is human, to arr is pirate."

Unknown

"Too bad the only people who know how to run the country are busy driving cabs and cutting hair."

George Burns (1896 - 1996), American comedian, actor, and writer.

"Too much of a good thing is wonderful."

Mae West (1893 - 1980), American actress, playwright, screenwriter and sex symbol.

"When you come to a fork in the road, take it."

Yogi Berra (1925 -), former American Major League Baseball player and manager. He played almost his entire 19-year baseball career (1946 - 1965) for the New York Yankees.

"While not exactly disgruntled, she was far from being gruntled."

Unknown

"Work is the ruin of the drinking classes."

Oscar Wilde (1854 - 1900), Irish dramatist, novelist and poet.

"You better know where you're going because if you don't, you might not get there."

Yogi Berra (1925 -), former American Major League Baseball player and manager. He played almost his entire 19-year baseball career (1946 - 1965) for the New York Yankees.

"You can observe a lot by watching."

Yogi Berra (1925 -), former American Major League Baseball player and manager. He played almost his entire 19-year baseball career (1946 - 1965) for the New York Yankees.

"You can tune a piano, but you can't tuna fish."

Album title from the band *REO Speedwagon*.

action agreement alligators believe better business
change dare decisions dependence discovery dream encourage
execution exploration failure feeling followers folly fools freedom
goals ideas ignore innovation inspire job leaders
leadership lies management
mistakes passion persuasion pessimism planning power praise
problem recognition retrospect risk selling ship speaking speech
statistics talking vision work

"A bad plan is better than no plan."

Unknown

"A genuine leader is not a searcher for consensus but a molder of consensus."

Martin Luther King Jr. (1929 - 1968), American civil rights leader and Nobel Peace Prize winner.

"A good plan, violently executed today, is better than a perfect plan tomorrow."

Bill Gates (1955 -), American business magnate, philanthropist, author. Best known for Co-Founding software company Microsoft.

"A leader is one who knows the way, goes the way and shows the way."

John C. Maxwell (1947 -), American evangelical Christian author, speaker, and pastor who has written more than 50 books, primarily focusing on leadership.

"A plan in your head isn't worth the paper it's written on."

Yogi Berra (1925 -), former American Major League Baseball player and manager. He played almost his entire 19-year baseball career (1946 - 1965) for the New York Yankees.

"A ship in harbor is safe, but that is not what ships are built for."

John A. Shedd

"Admit nothing, deny everything and make counter-accusations."

Unknown

"After all is said and done, more is said than done."

Aesop (620 BC - 560 BC), Ancient Greek fabulist and author of a collection of Greek fables.

"All work and no play will make you a manager."

Unknown

"Amateurs practice until they get it right, professionals practice so they won't get it wrong."

Unknown

"An invasion of armies can be resisted, but not an idea whose time has come."

Victor Hugo (1802 - 1885), French writer and poet. From "Histoire d'un Crime" (1852).

"Any supervisor worth his salt would rather deal with people who attempt too much than with those who try too little."

Lee Iacocca (1924 -), American businessman known for the unsuccessful Ford Pinto, being fired from Ford Motor Company, and his revival of the Chrysler Corporation in the 1980s.

"Be thankful for problems. If they were less difficult, someone with less ability might have your job."

James A. Lovell (1928 -), a former NASA astronaut and a retired captain in the US Navy, most famous as the commander of the Apollo 13 mission, which suffered a critical failure en route to the Moon but was brought back safely to Earth by the efforts of the crew and mission control.

"Before you can inspire with emotion, you must be swamped with it yourself. Before you can move their tears, your own must flow. To convince them, you must yourself believe."

Sir Winston Churchill (1874 - 1965), British orator, author and Prime Minister during World War II.

"Better to be bold and decisive and risk being wrong, than to ponder at length and be right too late."

Unknown

"Choose a job you like and you will never have to work a day of your life."

Confucius (551 - 479 BC), Chinese writer and philosopher.

"Coming together is a beginning, staying together is progress, and working together is success."

Henry Ford (1863 - 1947), prominent American industrialist, the founder of the Ford Motor Company, and sponsor of the development of the assembly line technique of mass production.

"Diplomacy is the art of telling someone to go to hell and having them look forward to the trip."

Unknown

"Discovery consists of seeing what everybody has seen and thinking what nobody has thought."

Albert Szent-Györgi (1893 - 1986), Hungarian physiologist who won the Nobel Prize in Medicine in 1937 and is credited with discovering vitamin C.

"Do what you do so well that people can't resist telling others about you."

Walt Disney (1901 - 1966), American film producer, director, screenwriter, voice actor, animator, entrepreneur, entertainer, international icon, and philanthropist. Disney is famous for his influence in the field of entertainment during the 20th century. As the Co-Founder (with his brother Roy O. Disney) of Walt Disney Productions, Disney became one of the best-known motion picture producers in the world. The corporation he co-founded, now known as The Walt Disney Company, today has annual revenues of approximately $35 billion.

"Don't be irreplaceable -- if you can't be replaced, you won't be promoted."

Unknown

"Don't confuse effort with results."

Unknown

"Don't tell a man how to do a thing. Tell him what you want done, and he'll surprise you with his ingenuity."

General George S. Patton Jr. (1885 - 1945), American Army officer best known for his leadership while commanding corps and armies as a general during World War II. He was also well known for his eccentricity and controversial outspokenness.

"Don't tell me how hard you work. Tell me how much you get done."

James Ling (1922 - 2004), American businessman.

"Failing to plan is planning to fail."

Alan Lakein, American author on personal time management.

"Far better it is to dare mighty things, to win glorious triumphs even though checkered by failure, than to rank with those timid spirits who neither enjoy nor suffer much because they live in the gray twilight that knows neither victory nor defeat."

Theodore Roosevelt (1858 - 1919), 26th US President (1901 - 1909).

"Flatter me, and I may not believe you. Criticize me, and I may not like you. Ignore me, and I may not forgive you. Encourage me, and I will not forget you."

William Arthur Ward (1921 - 1994), American writer of inspirational articles, poems and meditations.

"Freedom lies in being bold."

Robert Frost (1874 - 1963), American poet.

"Good communication does not mean that you have to speak in perfectly formed sentences and paragraphs. It isn't about slickness. Simple and clear go a long way."

John Kotter (1947 -), American Professor at the Harvard Business School and author, who is regarded as an authority on leadership and change.

"Good ideas are not adopted automatically. They must be driven into practice with courageous patience."

Hyman Rickover (1900 - 1986), a four-star admiral in the US Navy who directed the original development of naval nuclear propulsion and controlled its operations for three decades as director of Naval Reactors.

"Good leaders are like baseball umpires; they go practically unnoticed when doing their jobs right."

Byrd Baggett

"Hear and you forget; see and you remember; do and you understand."

Unknown

"If I had asked people what they wanted, they would have said faster horses."

Henry Ford (1863 - 1947), prominent American industrialist, the founder of the Ford Motor Company, and sponsor of the development of the assembly line technique of mass production.

"If my heart gets there first, it will be easy for my body to follow."

Paulo Coehlo (1947 -), Brazilian lyricist and novelist.

"If not now, when?"

Hillel (30 BC - 10 AD), Jewish scholar.

"If we are ever in doubt about what to do, it is a good rule of thumb to ask ourselves what we shall wish on the morrow that we had done."

Sir John Lubbock (1834 - 1913), English writer.

"If you aren't part of the solution, you're part of the problem."

Sydney J. Harris (1917 - 1986), London-born American journalist for the Chicago Daily News and later the Chicago Sun-Times. His column, "Strictly Personal," was syndicated in many newspapers throughout the US and Canada.

"If you can't state your position in eight words or less, you don't have a position."

Seth Godin (1960 -), American entrepreneur, author and public speaker. Godin popularized the topic of permission marketing.

"If you don't have a competitive advantage, don't compete."

Jack Welch (1935 -), American chemical engineer, businessman and author. He was Chairman and CEO of General Electric (1981 - 2001).

"If you want to go fast, go alone. If you want to go far, go with others."

Melinda Gates (1964 -), American philanthropist and wife of Bill Gates. She is the co-founder and co-chair of the Bill & Melinda Gates Foundation and a former unit manager for several Microsoft products such as Publisher, Microsoft Bob, Encarta, and Expedia.

"If you work just for the money, you'll never make it, but if you love what you're doing and you always put the customer first, success will be yours."

Ray Kroc (1902 - 1984), American businessman and Founder of McDonald's Corporation.

"If your actions inspire others to dream more, learn more, do more and become more, you are a leader."

John Quincy Adams (1767 - 1648), 6th US President (1825 - 1829).

"In any moment of decision, the best thing you can do is the right thing. The next best thing you can do is the wrong thing. The worst thing you can do is nothing."

Theodore Roosevelt (1858 - 1919), 26th US President (1901 - 1909).

"It is easier to get forgiveness than permission."

Rear Admiral Grace Hopper (1906 - 1992), American computer scientist and US Navy officer. A pioneer in the field, she was one of the first programmers of the Harvard Mark I computer, and developed the first compiler for a computer programming language.

"It is not the critic who counts; not the man who points out how the strong man stumbles, or where the doer of deeds could have done them better. The credit belongs to the man who is actually in the arena, whose face is marred by dust and sweat and blood, who strives valiantly; who errs and comes short again and again; because there is not effort without error and shortcomings; but who does actually strive to do the deed; who knows the great enthusiasm, the great devotion, who spends himself in a worthy cause, who at the best knows in the end the triumph of high achievement and who at the worst, if he fails, at least he fails while daring greatly. So that his place shall never be with those cold and timid souls who know neither victory nor defeat."

Theodore Roosevelt (1858 - 1919), 26th US President (1901 - 1909).

"It's better to be a company than to work for a company."

Jim Coudal, entrepreneur in a Keynote Speech at South By Southwest (SXSW) 2006.

"It's not who you know, it's who knows you."

Jeffrey Gitomer (1946 -), American author, professional speaker, and business trainer, who writes and lectures internationally on sales, customer loyalty, and personal development.

"I've learned that people will forget what you said, people will forget what you did, but people will never forget how you made them feel."

Maya Angelou (1928 -), American author and poet.

"I've never learned anything from someone who agreed with me."

Unknown

"Lead, follow, or get out of the way."

Thomas Paine (1737 - 1809), English-born writer and philosopher who played a significant role helping America in the American Revolution.

"Leaders are people who do the right thing; managers are people who do things right."

Warren G. Bennis (1925 -), American scholar, organizational consultant and author, widely regarded as a pioneer of the contemporary field of Leadership studies.

"Leaders think and talk about the solutions. Followers think and talk of the problems."

Brian Tracy (1944 -), Canadian self-help author who has recorded many of his works as audio books. His presentations and seminar topics include leadership, sales, managerial effectiveness, and business strategy.

"Leaders who can stay optimistic and upbeat, even under intense pressure, radiate the positive feelings that create resonance. By staying in control of their feelings and impulses, they craft an environment of trust, comforts and fairness. And that self-management has a trickle down effect from the leader."

Daniel Goleman (1946 -), American author, psychologist, and science journalist. For twelve years, he wrote for The New York Times, specializing in psychology and brain sciences. He is the author of more than 10 books on psychology, education, science, and leadership.

"Leadership is about capturing the imagination and enthusiasm of your people with clearly defined goals that cut through the fog like a beacon in the night."

Unknown

"Leadership is practiced not so much in words as in attitude and in actions."

Harold S. Geneen (1910 - 1997), American businessman.

"Leadership is the art of getting someone else to do something you want done because he wants to do it."

Dwight D. Eisenhower, General and 34th US President (1953 - 1961).

"Left to themselves, things tend to go from bad to worse."

One of Murphy's Laws.

"Make sure you have finished speaking before your audience has finished listening."

Dorothy Sarnoff (1914 - 2008), American operatic soprano, musical theatre actress, and self-help guru.

"Management works in the system; leadership works on the system."

Stephen R. Covey (1932 -), Professor and author best known for the best-selling book, "The Seven Habits of Highly Effective People."

"My rules for picking people: look for intelligence and judgment, and most critically a capacity to anticipate, to see around corners."

Colin Powell (1937 -), former Army General and US Secretary of State (2001 – 2005).

"Never doubt that a small group of thoughtful, committed citizens can change the world. Indeed, it's the only thing that ever has."

Margaret Mead (1901 - 1978), American cultural anthropologist.

"Never innovate to compete, innovate to change the rules of the game."

David O. Adeife

"Never let anyone tell you no who doesn't have the power to say yes."

Eleanor Roosevelt (1884 - 1962), 32nd US first lady (1933 - 1945), UN diplomat and humanitarian.

"No man ever listened himself out of a job."

Calvin Coolidge (1872 - 1933), 30th US President (1923 - 1929).

"No one who accomplished things could expect to avoid mistakes. Only those who do nothing make no mistakes."

Harry S. Truman, 33rd US President (1945 - 1953).

"No person can be a great leader unless he takes genuine joy in the success of those under him."

W.A. Nance

"Nothing succeeds like one's own successor."

Clarence H. Hinclcs

"Obstacles are what you see when you take your eyes off the goal."

Vince Lombardi (1913 - 1970), American football coach best known as the head coach of the Green Bay Packers during the 1960s.

"One doesn't discover new lands without consenting to lose sight of the shore for a very long time."

André Gide (1869 - 1951), French author and winner of the Nobel Prize in literature in 1947.

"Only hire people you'd be happy to have in your home and play poker with."

Dick Kress, former President at Norelco.

"Penny wise and pound foolish."

Unknown

"People and their managers are working so hard to be sure things are done right, that they hardly have time to decide if they are doing the right things."

Stephen R. Covey (1932 -), Professor and author best known for the best-selling book, "The Seven Habits of Highly Effective People."

"People are hungry... NO, starving, for praise and appreciation."

Unknown

"People don't want to be managed, they want to be led."

Lucy Ivins

"People forget how fast you did a job - but they remember how well you did it."

Howard W. Newton

"Pessimists complain about the wind. Optimists expect it to change. Leaders adjust the sails."

Unknown

"Plans may not work, but planning does."

Michael Moritz (1954 -), Welsh-American venture capitalist with Sequoia Capital in Menlo Park, California in Silicon Valley.

"Remember the difference between a Boss and a Leader, a Boss says "Go!" - a Leader says, "Let's go!""

F. M. Kelly

"Repetition does not transform a lie into a truth."

Franklin D. Roosevelt (1882 - 1945), 32nd US President (1933 - 1945).

"Satisfaction is the symptom of under performance."

Unknown

"Some people let things happen. Other people make things happen. Too many ask 'what happened?'"

Unknown

"Stand for something greater than your bottom line, and people will stand behind you."

Unknown

"Start with good people, lay out the rules, communicate with your employees, motivate them and reward them. If you do all those things effectively, you can't miss."

Lee Iacocca (1924 -), American businessman known for the unsuccessful Ford Pinto, being fired from Ford Motor Company, and his revival of the Chrysler Corporation in the 1980s.

"The ability, the will to win, the will to excel are all that matter. These are so much more important than the events that occur."

Vince Lombardi (1913 - 1970), American football coach best known as the head coach of the Green Bay Packers during the 1960s.

"The beatings will continue until morale improves."

Unknown

"The beginning is half of every action."

Greek proverb.

"The best leader is the one who has sense enough to pick good men to do what he wants done, and self-restraint enough to keep from meddling with them while they do it."

Theodore Roosevelt (1858 - 1919), 26th US President (1901 - 1909).

"The best thing a leader can do for a great group is to allow the members to discover their greatness."

Rear Admiral Grace Hopper (1906 - 1992), American computer scientist and US Navy officer. A pioneer in the field, she was one of the first programmers of the Harvard Mark I computer, and developed the first compiler for a computer programming language.

"The deepest human need is the need to be appreciated."

William James (1842 - 1910), a pioneering American psychologist and philosopher who was trained as a medical doctor. He wrote influential books on the young science of psychology, educational psychology, psychology of religious experience and mysticism, and on the philosophy of pragmatism.

"The distinction between a manager and a leader is as broad as the distance between control and inspiration."

Unknown

"The inherent vice of capitalism is the unequal sharing of the blessings. The inherent blessing of socialism is the equal sharing of misery."

Sir Winston Churchill (1874 - 1965), British orator, author and Prime Minister during World War II.

"The leaders who work most effectively, it seems to me, never say "I." And that's not because they have trained themselves not to say "I." They don't think "I." They think "we"; they think "team." They understand their job to be to make the team function. They accept responsibility and don't sidestep it, but "we" gets the credit. This is what creates trust, what enables you to get the task done."

Peter F. Drucker (1909 - 2006), American writer and management consultant.

"The mark of a good action is that it appears inevitable in retrospect."

Robert Louis Stevenson (1850 - 1894), Scottish writer.

"The only thing necessary for the triumph of evil is for good men to do nothing."

Edmund Burke (1729 - 1797), Irish statesman, author, orator, political theorist, and philosopher.

"The only things that evolve by themselves in an organization are disorder, friction and malperformance."

Peter F. Drucker (1909 - 2006), American writer and management consultant.

"The profit and loss account of a company can be compared with a bikini; what it shows is interesting, but what it hides is essential."

Unknown

"The right word may be effective, but no word was ever as effective as a rightly timed pause."

Mark Twain, the pen name of Samuel Langhorne Clemens (1835 – 1910), American writer and humorist.

"The secret of all victory lies in the organization of the non-obvious."

Marcus Aurelius (~ 121 AD - 180 AD), Roman Emperor (161 AD - 180 AD) and philosopher.

"The time to stop talking is when the other person nods his head affirmatively but says nothing."

Henry S. Haskins

"The two most powerful things in existence: a kind word and a thoughtful gesture."

Ken Langone (~ 1935 -), American venture capitalist, investment banker and financial backer of The Home Depot.

"The ultimate result of shielding men from the effects of folly is to fill the world with fools."

Herbert Spencer (1820 - 1903), English philosopher.

"The very essence of leadership is that you have a vision. It's got to be a vision you can articulate clearly and forcefully on every occasion. You can't blow an uncertain trumpet."

Theodore Hesburgh (1917 -), priest and President Emeritus of the University of Notre Dame.

"The way to get started is to stop talking and start doing."

Walt Disney (1901 - 1966), American film producer, director, screenwriter, voice actor, animator, entrepreneur, entertainer, international icon, and philanthropist. Disney is famous for his influence in the field of entertainment during the 20th century. As the Co-Founder (with his brother Roy O. Disney) of Walt Disney Productions, Disney became one of the best-known motion picture producers in the world. The corporation he co-founded, now known as The Walt Disney Company, today has annual revenues of approximately $35 billion.

"There are three kinds of lies: Lies, Damn Lies, and Statistics."

Benjamin Disraeli (1804 - 1881), British Prime Minister, parliamentarian, Conservative statesman and literary figure.

"There are two things that people want more than sex and money – recognition and praise."

Mary Kay Ash (1918 - 2001), American businesswoman and Founder of Mary Kay Cosmetics.

"There is one thing stronger than all the armies in the world, and that is an idea whose time has come."

Victor Hugo (1802 - 1885), French writer and poet.

"They may forget what you said, but they will never forget how you made them feel."

Carl W. Buechner

"Think like a man of action, act like a man of thought."

Henri Bergson (1859 - 1941), French philosopher and winner of the Nobel Prize in Literature (1927).

"To accomplish great things, we must not only act, but also dream; not only plan, but believe."

Anatole France (1844 - 1924), French poet, journalist, and novelist.

"To be a success in business, be daring, be first, be different."

Marchant

"To lead the people, walk behind them."

Lao-Tzu, mystic philosopher of ancient China, and best known as the author of the "Tao Te Ching". His association with the "Tao Te Ching" has led him to be traditionally considered the founder of Taoism (also spelled "Daoism").

"Vision is the art of seeing what is invisible to others."

Jonathan Swift (1667 - 1745), Anglo-Irish satirist, essayist, political pamphleteer, poet and cleric. He is remembered for works such as "Gulliver's Travels."

"Vision without execution is hallucination."

Thomas Edison (1847 - 1931), American inventor and salesman.

"We have to be prepared to lose sight of the shore to see the ocean."

Unknown

"We haven't failed. We know a thousand things that won't work, so we're that much closer to finding what will."

Thomas Edison (1847 - 1931), American inventor and salesman.

"We must either find a way or make one."

Hannibal (247 BC - 183 BC), Carthaginian General known for his battles against the Romans.

"We need men who can dream of things that never were."

John F. Kennedy (1917 - 1963), 35th US President (1961 - 1963) from a speech in Dublin, Ireland, June 28, 1963.

"We should be taught not to wait for inspiration to start a thing. Action always generates inspiration. Inspiration seldom generates action."

Frank Tibolt

"Well done is better than well said."

Benjamin Franklin (1706 - 1790), American statesman, scientist, writer and printer.

"What business entrepreneurs are to the economy, social entrepreneurs are to social change. They are driven, creative individuals who question the status quo, exploit new opportunities, refuse to give up, and remake the world for the better."

David Bornstein, American journalist and author who specializes in writing about social innovation. He has written three books on social entrepreneurship. He is the founder of Dowser.org, a news site that reports on social innovation.

"When all is said and done, MUCH more will have been said than done."

Lou Holtz (1937-1980), American football coach.

"When two men in business always agree, one of them is unnecessary."

William Wrigley Jr. (1861 - 1932), American industrialist who founded chewing gum giant Wm. Wrigley Jr. Company in 1891.

"When you have an important point to make, don't try to be subtle or clever. Use a pile driver. Hit the point once. Then come back and hit it again. Then hit it a third time - a tremendous whack."

Sir Winston Churchill (1874 - 1965), British orator, author and Prime Minister during World War II.

"When you're up to your ass in alligators, it's hard to remember that your goal was to drain the swamp."

Unknown

"Whenever you see a successful business, someone once made a courageous decision."

Peter F. Drucker (1909 - 2006), American writer and management consultant.

"With B team players, there is no limit to what you can't do."

Radoslav Danilak, startup entrepreneur.

"Worry about being better; bigger will take care of itself."

Gary Comer (1929 – 2006), American entrepreneur and Founder of Lands' End.

"Yesterday is gone. Tomorrow has not yet come. We have only today. Let us begin."

Mother Teresa (1910 - 1997), Albanian missionary and Nobel Peace Prize winner.

"You can't build a reputation on what you are going to do."

Henry Ford (1863 - 1947), prominent American industrialist, the founder of the Ford Motor Company, and sponsor of the development of the assembly line technique of mass production.

"You can't catch the big fish by skimming the surface."

Unknown

"You can't do today's job with yesterday methods and still be in business tomorrow."

Unknown

"You don't have to be a person of influence to be influential. In fact, the most influential people in my life are probably not even aware of the things they've taught me."

Scott Adams (1957 -), American creator of the Dilbert comic strip and the author of several nonfiction works of satire, commentary, business, and general speculation.

"You don't have to explain something you never said."

Unknown

"You don't have to hold a position in order to be a leader."

Anthony D'Angelo Founder of The Collegiate EmPowerment Company and creator of "The Inspiration Book" series.

"You don't lead by hitting people over the head... that's assault."

Dwight D. Eisenhower, General and 34th US President (1953 - 1961).

"You'll never plough a field turning it over in your mind."

Irish Proverb.

"Your lack of planning doesn't constitute an emergency on my part."

Harried office workers around the world.

ability advice application apply beauty books brains classic collaboration commitment
conclusion creative decency discovery dress education expression failure
focus fool genius ignorance imagination inquiries instructions integrity
intellectual intelligent kindness knowledge
learning lessons life listen living mistakes money
relearn reports school speak strength stupidity t-shirts teachers
teaching thinking university unlearn wisdom

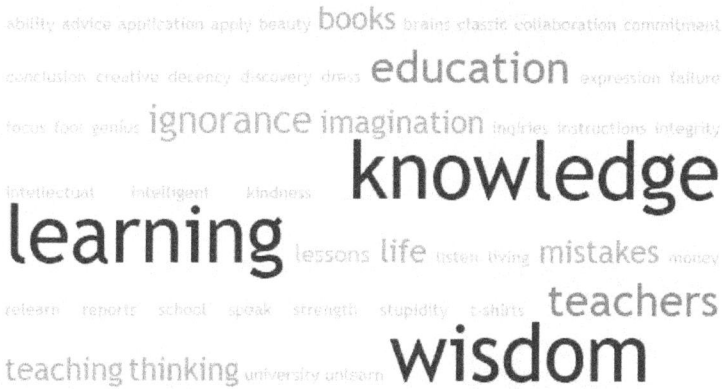

"A book is a gift you can open again and again."

Garrison Keillor (1942 -), American writer and broadcaster.

"A classic is something that everybody wants to have read and nobody has."

Mark Twain, the pen name of Samuel Langhorne Clemens (1835 – 1910), American writer and humorist.

"A conclusion is the place where you get tired of thinking."

Arthur Block

"A fellow who is always declaring he's no fool usually has his suspicions."

Wilson Mizner (1876 - 1933), American playwright, raconteur, and entrepreneur.

"A man who does not read good books does not have any advantage over the person who cannot read them."

Mark Twain, the pen name of Samuel Langhorne Clemens (1835 – 1910), American writer and humorist.

"A smart man knows what to say. But a wise man knows whether or not to say it."

Unknown

"A university is what a college becomes when the faculty loses interest in students."

John Ciardi (1916 - 1986), American poet.

"All human wisdom is summed up in two words - wait and hope."

Alexandre Dumas (1802-1870), French writer, who was one of the most prolific and most popular authors of the 19th century.

"All I really need to know about how to live and what to do and how to be I learned in kindergarten. Remember the Dick-and-Jane books and the first word you learned -- the biggest word of all -- look."

Robert Fulghum (1937 -), American author, painter, sculptor and former minister.

"All of the top achievers I know are life-long learners... Looking for new skills, insights, and ideas. If they're not learning, they're not growing... not moving toward excellence."

Denis Waitley (1933 -), American motivational speaker and writer, consultant and best-selling author.

"All true wisdom is found on T-shirts."

Unknown

"An intellectual is a man who takes more words than necessary to tell more than he knows."

Dwight D. Eisenhower, American Army General and 34th US President (1953 - 1961).

"As much as we need a prosperous economy, we also need a prosperity of kindness and decency."

Caroline Kennedy (1957 -), American author and attorney and a member of the influential Kennedy family.

"At age 20 we worry about what others think of us. At 40 we don't care what they think of us. At 60 we discover they haven't been thinking of us at all."

Ann Landers, a pen name created by Chicago Sun-Times advice columnist Ruth Crowley in 1943 and taken over by Eppie Lederer in 1955.

"Books were my pass to personal freedom. I learned to read at age three, and soon discovered there was a whole world to conquer that went beyond our farm in Mississippi."

Oprah Winfrey (1954 -), American television host, actress, producer, and philanthropist, best known for her self-titled, multi-award winning talk show, which has become the highest-rated program of its kind in history. She has been ranked the richest African American of the 20th century, the greatest black philanthropist in American history, and was once the world's only black billionaire. She is also, according to some assessments, the most influential woman in the world.

"Earth and sky, woods and fields, lakes and rivers, the mountain and the sea, are excellent schoolmasters, and teach some of us more than we can ever learn from books."

Sir John Lubbock (1834 - 1913), English biologist and politician.

"Education is learning what you didn't even know you didn't know."

Daniel J. Boorstin (1914 -), American social historian and educator.

"Give a jackass an education and you get a smartass."

Unknown

"Give a man a fish and he won't starve for a day. Teach a man how to fish and he won't starve for his entire life."

African proverb.

"I hope our wisdom will grow with our power, and teach us that the less we use our power the greater it will be."

Thomas Jefferson (1743 - 1826), 3rd US President (1801 - 1809) and the primary writer of the Declaration of Independence in 1776.

"I never teach my pupils; I only attempt to provide the conditions in which they can learn."

Albert Einstein (1879 - 1955), German-born American physicist who developed the theories of relativity and won the Nobel Prize for Physics in 1921.

"I not only use all the brains that I have, but all that I can borrow."

Woodrow Wilson (1856 - 1924), 28th US President (1913 - 1921). He served during World War I and was a driving force behind the creation of the League of Nations.

"If everything else fails, read the instructions."

Unknown

"If you can't explain it simply, you don't understand it well enough."

Albert Einstein (1879 - 1955), German-born American physicist who developed the theories of relativity and won the Nobel Prize for Physics in 1921.

"If you have an apple and I have an apple and we exchange these apples then you and I will still each have one apple. But if you have an idea and I have an idea and we exchange these ideas, then each of us will have two ideas."

George Bernard Shaw (1856 - 1950), Irish writer and playwright who won the 1925 Nobel Prize for Literature.

"If you lose do not lose the lesson."

Tenzin Gyatso (1935 -), Tibetan Buddhist leader and the 14th Dalai Lama. He won the Nobel Peace Prize in 1989, and is also well known for his lifelong advocacy for Tibetans inside and outside Tibet.

"If you think education is expensive, try ignorance."

Derek Bok (1930 -), American lawyer, educator and the former president of Harvard University.

"Imagination is intelligence having fun."

Unknown

"Imagination is more important than knowledge. For knowledge is limited to all we now know and understand, while imagination embraces the entire world, and all there ever will be to know and understand."

Albert Einstein (1879 - 1955), German-born American physicist who developed the theories of relativity and won the Nobel Prize for Physics in 1921.

"Imagination was given to man to compensate him for what he isn't; and a sense of humor to console him for what he is."

Unknown

"In the end we retain from our studies only that which we practically apply."

Johann Wolfgang von Goethe (1749 - 1832), German writer, philosopher and scientist.

"It is the province of knowledge to speak, and it is the province of wisdom to listen."

Oliver Wendell Holmes (1809 - 1894), American physician, poet, writer, humorist and Professor at Harvard.

"It is the supreme art of the teacher to awaken joy in creative expression and knowledge."

Albert Einstein (1879 - 1955), German-born American physicist who developed the theories of relativity and won the Nobel Prize for Physics in 1921.

"Knowing is not enough; we must apply. Willing is not enough; we must do."

Johann Wolfgang von Goethe (1749 - 1832), German writer, philosopher and scientist.

"Knowing others is intelligence; knowing yourself is true wisdom. Mastering others is strength; mastering yourself is true power."

Lao-Tzu, mystic philosopher of ancient China, and best known as the author of the "Tao Te Ching". His association with the "Tao Te Ching" has led him to be traditionally considered the founder of Taoism (also spelled "Daoism").

"Knowledge is a process of piling up facts; wisdom lies in their simplification."

Martin H. Fischer

"Knowledge is modest, cautious and pure; ignorance is boastful, conceited and sure."

Unknown

"Learn from the mistakes of others. You can't live long enough to make them all yourself."

Eleanor Roosevelt (1884 - 1962), 32nd US first lady (1933 - 1945), UN diplomat and humanitarian.

"Learning from your mistakes is smart, learning from the mistakes of others is wise."

Unknown

"Mistakes are the portals of discovery."

James Joyce (1882 - 1941), Irish novelist and poet, considered to be one of the most influential writers in the modernist avant-garde of the early 20th century. Joyce is best known for "Ulysses" (1922), a landmark novel which perfected his stream of consciousness technique and combined nearly every literary device available in a modern re-telling of "The Odyssey."

"Money glitters, beauty sparkles, and intelligence shines."

Unknown

"My education was interrupted only by my schooling."

Sir Winston Churchill (1874 - 1965), British orator, author and Prime Minister during World War II.

"Never mistake knowledge for wisdom. One helps you make a living; the other helps you make a life."

Sandra Carey

"Nothing is more terrible than ignorance in action."

Johann Wolfgang von Goethe (1749 - 1832), German writer, philosopher and scientist.

"One's work may be finished someday, but one's education, never."

Alexandre Dumas (1802 - 1870), French writer. His novels, including "The Count of Monte Cristo" and "The Three Musketeers."

"People don't care how much you know, but they know how much you care by the way you listen."

Bob Conklin

"School is a building that has four walls -- with tomorrow inside."

Lon Watters

"Sometimes I think the surest sign that intelligent life exists elsewhere in the universe is that none of it has tried to contact us."

Bill Watterson (1958 -), American cartoonist best known for his popular comic strip "Calvin and Hobbes."

"Student: 'How long do you want this report to be?' Teacher: 'I would like you to think of this paper much like a lady's dress - long enough to cover the subject, yet short enough to keep it interesting.'"

Unknown

"Teachers open the door, but you must enter by yourself."

Chinese proverb.

"Tell me, and I will forget. Show me, and I may remember. Involve me, and I will understand."

Confucius (551 BC - 479 BC), Chinese writer and philosopher.

"The best compliment to a child or a friend is the feeling you give him that he has been set free to make his own inquiries, to come to conclusions that are right for him, whether or not they coincide with your own."

Alistair Cooke (1908 - 2004), British/American journalist, television personality and broadcaster.

"The cost of educating a child today is immense. But the cost of not educating a child is incalculable."

Unknown

"The difference between stupidity and genius is that genius has its limits."

Albert Einstein (1879 - 1955), German-born American physicist who developed the theories of relativity and won the Nobel Prize for Physics in 1921.

"The fool wonders, the wise man asks."

Benjamin Disraeli (1804 - 1881), British Prime Minister, parliamentarian, Conservative statesman and literary figure.

"The illiterate of the 21st century will not be those who cannot read and write, but those who cannot learn, unlearn, and relearn."

Alvin Toffler (1928 -), American writer and futurist.

"The important thing is not so much that every child should be taught, as that every child should be given the wish to learn."

Sir John Lubbock (1834-1913), English biologist and politician.

"The level of thinking that got us here is going to have to be exceeded to get us out of here."

Albert Einstein (1879 - 1955), German-born American physicist who developed the theories of relativity and won the Nobel Prize for Physics in 1921.

"The mediocre teacher tells. The good teacher explains. The superior teacher demonstrates. The great teacher inspires."

William Arthur Ward (1921 - 1994), American writer of inspirational articles, poems and meditations.

"The purpose of education is to replace an empty mind with an open one."

Malcolm S. Forbes (1919 - 1990), American publisher of *Forbes* magazine.

"The purpose of learning is growth, and our minds, unlike our bodies, can continue growing as long as we live."

Mortimer Adler (1902 - 2001), American philosopher, educator and editor.

"To accept good advice is but to increase one's own ability."

Johann Wolfgang von Goethe (1749 - 1832), German writer, philosopher and scientist.

"To acquire knowledge, one must study; but to acquire wisdom, one must observe."

Marilyn vos Savant (1946 -), American magazine columnist, author, lecturer, and playwright who rose to fame through her listing in the Guinness Book of World Records under "Highest IQ".

"We can't solve problems by using the same kind of thinking we used when we created them."

Albert Einstein (1879 - 1955), German-born American physicist who developed the theories of relativity and won the Nobel Prize for Physics in 1921.

"What they lack in intelligence they make up for in ignorance."

Unknown

"What wisdom can you find that is greater than kindness?"

Jean-Jacques Rousseau (1712-1778), French philosopher and writer whose novels inspired the leaders of the French Revolution.

"Wisdom is knowing the right path to take.... Integrity...is taking it."

MH McKee

"You know more than you think you do. You can do more than you think you can."

Unknown

"Your ability to learn faster than your competition is your only sustainable competitive advantage."

Arie de Geus (1930 -), Dutch businessman.

acceptance accomplishment achievement action adaptation aging beginning

courage death decision deeds depth dream experience faith

focus fool future god happy imagination important jobs joy

learning life live love matter meaning mistakes moments

parenting passion path people perspective problem purpose questions

rainbow reaction regret religion soul television tv useful wise young

"A city is a large community where people are lonesome together."

Herbert Prochnow (1897 - 1998), American banking executive, noted toastmaster and author.

"A proverb is a short sentence based on long experience."

Miguel de Cervantes (1547 - 1616), Spanish novelist, poet, and playwright. His magnum opus "Don Quixote," considered the first modern novel, is a classic of Western literature, and is regarded amongst the best works of fiction ever written.

"A religious war is like children fighting over who has the strongest imaginary friend."

Unknown

"A single conversation with a wise man is better than ten years of study."

Chinese proverb.

"A wise man sees as much as he should, not as much as he can."

Unknown

"A wise person has something to say, a fool has to say something."

Unknown

"Advice is what we ask for when we already know the answer but wish we didn't."

Erica Jong (1942 -), American author and teacher.

"Age is a case of mind over matter. If you don't mind, it don't matter."

Leroy Robert "Satchel" Paige (1906 - 1983), pitcher for the Pittsburgh Crawfords and the Kansas City Monarchs of the Negro Leagues; Cleveland Indians, St. Louis Browns and Kansas City Athletics of MLB (1926-53, 1965), Hall of Fame (1971).

"All the great things are simple, and many can be expressed in a single word: freedom; justice; honor; duty; mercy; hope."

Sir Winston Churchill (1874 - 1965), British orator, author and Prime Minister during World War II.

"And in the end, it's not the years in your life that count. It's the life in your years."

Abraham Lincoln (1809 - 1865), 16th US President. His term of office was from 1861 to 1865 and included the American Civil War.

"And remember, no matter where you go, there you are."

Earl Mac Rauch, from the movie "Buckaroo Banzai."

"Anything in life worth having takes time, commitment and focus."

Unknown

"Art washes away from the soul, the dust of everyday life."

Pablo Picasso (1881 - 1973), Spanish painter, draughtsman, and sculptor who lived most of his adult life in France. He is best known for co-founding the Cubist movement.

"Be a good ancestor. Stand for something bigger than yourself. Add value to the Earth during your sojourn."

Marian Wright Edelman (1939 -) American activist and founder of the Children's Defense Fund.

"Be aware of wonder. Live a balanced life - learn some and think some and draw and paint and sing and dance and play and work every day some."

Robert Fulghum (1937 -), American author, painter, sculptor and former minister.

"Beautiful young people are acts of nature, but beautiful old people are works of art."

Unknown

"Beginnings are usually scary and endings are usually sad, but it's everything in between that makes it all worth living."

Sandra Bullock (1964 -), American movie actress. From the movie "Hope Floats."

"Believe that things will work somehow out... follow your intuition and curiosity... trust your heart even when it leads you off the well-worn path... You have to trust that the dots will somehow connect in your future... The only way to do great work is to love what you do. If you haven't found it yet, keep looking. Don't settle. As with all matters of the heart, you'll know when you find it... Have the courage to follow your heart and intuition. They somehow already know what you truly want to become. Everything else is secondary."

Steve Jobs (1955 -), American businessman and Co-Founder at Apple Inc., the inventor of Mac computers, iPods, iPhones and iPads.

"By the time you learn the rules of life, you're too old to play the game."

Unknown

"Dance as though no one is watching. Love as though you've never been hurt. Sing as though no one can hear you. Live as though heaven is on earth."

Souza

"Death is more universal than life; everyone dies but not everyone lives."

A. Sachs

"Do not go where the path may lead go instead where there is no path and leave a trail."

Ralph Waldo Emerson (1803 - 1882), American writer and poet.

"Don't be pushed by your problems. Be led by your dreams."

Unknown

"Don't go around saying the world owes you a living. The world owes you nothing. It was here first."

Mark Twain, the pen name of Samuel Langhorne Clemens (1835 – 1910), American writer and humorist.

"Don't just seize the day - seize the rest of your life!"

Unknown

"Don't let your last thought be - 'I wish I had..........'"

Unknown

"Don't run through life so fast that you forget not only where you've been but also where you're going."

Unknown

"Don't spend time beating on a wall, hoping to transform it into a door."

Dr. Laura Schlessinger (1947 -), American talk radio host, socially conservative commentator and author.

"Don't take life too seriously, you'll never get out of it alive."

Elbert Hubbard (1856 - 1915), American writer and editor.

"Dream as if you would live forever; live as if you would die tomorrow."

James Dean (1931 - 1955), American film actor. He is a cultural icon, best embodied in the title of his most celebrated film, "Rebel Without a Cause" (1955), in which he starred as troubled Los Angeles teenager Jim Stark. The other two roles that defined his stardom were as loner Cal Trask in "East of Eden" (1955), and as the surly farmer, Jett Rink, in "Giant" (1956). His premature death in a car crash cemented his legendary status.

"Every fool knows that he cannot reach the stars but it never keeps a wise man from trying."

Ronnie B. Woods

"Every man dies, but not every man truly lives."

Sir William Wallace (~ 1272 - 1305), Scottish knight and landowner who became one of the main leaders during the Wars of Scottish Independence.

"Every morning in Africa, a gazelle wakes up. It knows it must run faster than the fastest lion or it will be killed. Every morning in Africa, a lion wakes up. It knows it must out run the slowest gazelle or it will starve to death. It does not matter whether you are a lion or a gazelle. When the sun comes up, you'd better be running."

Unknown

"Everyone Is a prisoner of his own experiences. No one can eliminate prejudices - just recognize them."

Edward R. Murrow (1908 - 1965), American broadcast journalist. From a television broadcast December 31, 1955.

"Experience is a hard teacher because she gives the test first, the lesson afterwards."

Vernon Sanders Law (1930 -), American and a retired Major League Baseball pitcher. He played for 16 seasons (1950-1951 and 1954-1967) for the Pittsburgh Pirates.

"Experience is something you don't get until just after you need it."

Steven Wright (1955 -), American comedian, actor and writer.

"Experience is that marvelous thing that enables you recognize a mistake when you make it again."

Earl Wilson

"Experience is the name everyone gives to their mistakes."

Oscar Wilde (1854 - 1900), Irish dramatist, novelist and poet.

"Experience taught me a few things. One is to listen to your gut, no matter how good something sounds on paper. The second is that you're generally better off sticking with what you know. And the third is that sometimes your best investments are the ones you don't make."

Donald Trump (1946 -), American business magnate, socialite, author, and television personality.

"Fair is where they put ribbons on pigs."

Unknown

"Faithless is he who quits when the road darkens."

J.R.R. Tolkien (1892 - 1973), English writer, poet, philologist, and university professor, best known as the author of the classic high fantasy works "The Hobbit", "The Lord of the Rings", and "The Silmarillion."

"Favorite people, favorite places, favorite memories of the past. . .these are the joys of a lifetime. . .these are the things that last."

Unknown

"Following the path of least resistance makes rivers and men crooked."

Francis Gray

"Fool me once, shame on you; fool me twice, shame on me."

Unknown

"Fools look to tomorrow, wise men use tonight."

Scottish proverb.

"For those who believe, no proof is necessary; for those who don't believe, no proof is possible."

Stuart Chase (1888 - 1985), American economist and engineer trained at MIT. His writings covered topics as diverse as general semantics and physical economy. His hybrid background of engineering and economics places him in the same philosophical camp as R. Buckminster Fuller.

"From what we get, we can make a living; what we give, however, makes a life."

Arthur Ashe (1943 - 1993), American professional tennis player.

"God doesn't discriminate ... only religions do."

Unknown

"Good judgment comes from experience. Experience comes from bad judgment."

Unknown

"Growing old isn't so bad when you consider the alternative."

Maurice Chevalier (1888 - 1972), French actor, singer, and popular vaudeville entertainer.

"Happiness lies in the joy of achievement and the thrill of creative effort."

Franklin D. Roosevelt (1882 - 1945), 32nd US President (1933 - 1945).

"Having someplace to go to is a home. Having someone to love is family. Having both is a blessing."

Unknown

"He who asks is a fool for five minutes, but he who does not ask remains a fool forever."

Chinese proverb.

"History is written by the victors."

Sir Winston Churchill (1874 - 1965), British orator, author and Prime Minister during World War II.

"I believe in the small of a woman's back, the hanging curve ball, high fiber, good scotch, that the novels of Susan Sontag are self-indulgent, overrated crap. I believe Lee Harvey Oswald acted alone. I believe there ought to be a constitutional amendment outlawing Astroturf and the designated hitter. I believe in the sweet spot, soft-core pornography, opening your presents Christmas morning rather Christmas Eve and I believe in long, slow, deep, soft, wet kisses that last three days."

Crash Davis (played by Kevin Costner) In the movie "Bull Durham."

"I believe that imagination is stronger than knowledge - myth is more potent than history - dreams are more powerful than facts - hope always triumphs over experience - laughter is the cure for grief – love is stronger than death."

Robert Fulghum (1937 -), American author, painter, sculptor and former minister.

"I cannot believe that the purpose of life is to be "happy." I think the purpose of life is to be useful, to be responsible, to be compassionate. It is above all to matter, to count, to stand for something, to have made some difference that you lived at all!"

Leo Rosten (1908 - 1997), Russian-born (in an area now part of Poland), teacher and academic. He is best known as a humorist in the fields of scriptwriting, story writing, journalism and Yiddish lexicography.

"I don't want to get to the end of my life and find that I just lived the length of it. I want to have lived the width of it as well."

Diane Ackerman (1948 -), American author, poet, and naturalist known best for her work "A Natural History of the Senses."

"I have a great ambition to die of exhaustion rather than boredom."

Thomas Carlyle (1795 - 1881), Scottish satirical writer, essayist, historian and teacher during the Victorian era.

"I have never understood why women love cats. Cats are independent, they don't listen, they don't come in when you call, they like to stay out all night, and when they're home they like to be left alone and sleep. In other words, every quality that women hate in a man, they love in a cat."

Unknown

"I want to be all used up when I die."

George Bernard Shaw (1856 - 1950), Irish writer and playwright who won the 1925 Nobel Prize for Literature.

"I'd rather regret the things I've done than regret the things I haven't done."

Lucille Ball (1911 - 1989), American comedian, film, television, stage and radio actress, model, film and television executive, and star of sitcoms like "I Love Lucy."

"If I had my life to live over I would have cried and laughed less while watching television - and more while watching life."

Erma Bombeck (1927 - 1996), American humorist who achieved great popularity for her newspaper column that described suburban home life from the mid-1960s until the late 1990s. Bombeck also published 15 books, most of which became best-sellers.

"If I had to live my life again, I'd make the same mistakes, only sooner."

Tallulah Bankhead (1903 - 1968), American actress, talk-show host, and *bonne vivante*.

"If there is no passion in your life, then have you really lived? Find your passion, whatever it may be. Become it, and let it become you and you will find great things happen FOR you, TO you and BECAUSE of you."

T. Alan Armstrong

"If you are going through hell - keep going."

Sir Winston Churchill (1874 - 1965), British orator, author and Prime Minister during World War II.

"If you are not committing any sins, you are probably not having a lot of fun."

Unknown

"If you can imagine it, you can achieve it. If you can dream it, you can become it."

William Arthur Ward (1921 - 1994), American writer of inspirational articles, poems and meditations.

"If you don't set a baseline standard for what you'll accept in life, you'll find it's easy to slip into behaviors and attitudes or a quality of life that's far below what you deserve."

Anthony Robbins (1960 -), American self-help author and success coach. His books include "Unlimited Power: The New Science of Personal Achievement" and "Awaken the Giant Within".

"Imagination is everything. It is the preview of life's coming attractions."

Albert Einstein (1879 - 1955), German-born American physicist who developed the theories of relativity and won the Nobel Prize for Physics in 1921.

"In spite of everything I still believe that people are really good people at heart."

Anne Frank (1929 - 1945), one of the most renowned and most discussed Jewish victims of the Holocaust. Acknowledged for the quality of her writing, her diary has become one of the world's most widely read books, and has been the basis for several plays and films.

"In the final analysis, our most basic common link is that we all inhabit this small planet. We all breathe the same air. We all cherish our children's future. And we are all mortal."

John F. Kennedy (1917 - 1963), 35th US President (1961 - 1963).

"In three words I can sum up everything I've learned about life: it goes on."

Robert Frost (1874 - 1963), American poet.

"It is amazing what you can accomplish if you do not care who gets the credit."

Harry S. Truman, 33rd US President (1945 - 1953).

"It is better to wear out than to rust out."

Richard Cumberland (1631 - 1718), English philosopher and Bishop of Peterborough from 1691.

"It is during our darkest moments that we must focus to see the light."

Aristotle Onassis (1906 - 1975), prominent Greek shipping magnate.

"It is no profit to have learned well, if you neglect to do well."

Publilius Syrus, Latin writer of maxims, flourished in the 1st century BC. He was a Syrian who was brought as a slave to Italy, but by his wit and talent he won the favor of his master, who freed and educated him.

"It is not death that a man should fear, but he should fear never beginning to live."

Marcus Aurelius (~ 121 AD - 180 AD), Roman Emperor (161 AD - 180 AD) and philosopher.

"It is not how many years we live, but what we do with them. It is not what we receive, but what we give to others."

Evangeline Booth (1865 - 1950), British. She was the 4th General of the Salvation Army (1934 - 1939) and its first female General.

"It is not length of life, but depth of life."

Ralph Waldo Emerson (1803 - 1882), American writer and poet.

"It is not the strongest, swiftest, most ferocious who survive. It is the most adaptable."

Charles Darwin (1809 - 1882), English naturalist. He established that all species of life have descended over time from common ancestry, and proposed the scientific theory that this branching pattern of evolution resulted from a process that he called natural selection.

"It is not what we get. But who we become, what we contribute... that gives meaning to our lives."

Anthony Robbins (1960 -), American self-help author and success coach. His books include "Unlimited Power: The New Science of Personal Achievement" and "Awaken the Giant Within."

"It's a funny thing about life: if you refuse to accept anything but the best, you very often get it."

Thomas Dismukes

"It's better to burn out than it is to rust."

Neil Young (1945 -), Canadian singer-songwriter who is widely regarded as one of the most influential musicians of his generation.

"It's not that I'm afraid to die, I just don't want to be there when it happens."

Woody Allen (1935 -), American screenwriter, director, actor, comedian, jazz musician, author, and playwright. Allen's distinctive films, which run the gamut from dramas to screwball sex comedies, have made him a notable American director. From the movie "Without Feathers" (1976).

"I've always thought anyone can make money. Making a life worth living, that's the real test."

Robert Fulghum (1937 -), American author, painter, sculptor and former minister.

"I've learned that mistakes can often be as good a teacher as success."

Jack Welch (1935 -), American chemical engineer, businessman and author. He was Chairman and CEO of General Electric (1981 - 2001).

"Learn from yesterday, live for today, hope for tomorrow. The important thing is not to stop questioning."

Albert Einstein (1879 - 1955), German-born American physicist who developed the theories of relativity and won the Nobel Prize for Physics in 1921.

"Life begets life. Energy creates energy. It is by spending oneself that one becomes rich."

Sarah Bernhardt (1844 - 1923), French actress and writer.

"Life can only be understood backwards; but it must be lived forwards."

Sören Kierkegaard (1813 - 1855), Danish philosopher, theologian and author.

"Life is a banquet, and most poor suckers are starving to death!"

From the play "Auntie Mame."

"Life is a compromise of what your ego wants to do, what experience tells you to do, and what your nerves let you do."

Bruce Crampton (1935 -), Australian professional golfer.

"Life is a great big canvas; throw all the paint on it you can."

Danny Kaye (1913 - 1987), American actor, singer, dancer, and comedian.

"Life is a series of commas, not periods."

Matthew McConaughey (1969 -), American actor.

"Life is a succession of lessons, which must be lived to be understood."

Ralph Waldo Emerson (1803 - 1882), American writer and poet.

"Life is about making complicated things simple, and NOT simple things complicated."

Unknown

"Life is all about ass; you're either covering it, laughing it off, kicking it, kissing it, busting it, trying to get a piece of it, behaving like one – or you live with one!"

Unknown

"Life is like a game of cards. The hand you are dealt is determinism; the way you play it is free will."

Jawaharlal Nehru (1889 - 1964), Indian statesman who was the first and longest-serving Prime Minister of India (1947 - 1964).

"Life is like a grammar lesson. You find the past perfect and the present tense."

Unknown

"Life is no brief candle to me. It is a sort of splendid torch, which I have got a hold of for the moment; and I want to make it burn as brightly as possible before handing it on to future generations."

George Bernard Shaw (1856 - 1950), Irish writer and playwright who won on the 1925 Nobel Prize for Literature.

"Life is not about waiting for the storm to pass … it is about learning to dance in the rain."

Vivian Greene

"Life is not measured by the number of breaths we take, but the number of moments that take our breath away."

Maya Angelou (1928 -), American author and poet.

"Life is short, make it wide."

Spanish proverb.

"Life is too important to be taken seriously."

Oscar Wilde (1854 - 1900), Irish dramatist, novelist and poet.

"Life is too short to drink bad wine."

Unknown

"Life is too short to spend your precious time trying to convince a person who wants to live in gloom and doom otherwise. Give lifting that person your best shot, but don't hang around long enough for his or her bad attitude to pull you down. Instead, surround yourself with optimistic people."

Zig Ziglar (1926 -), American author, salesman, and motivational speaker.

"Life is what happens while you are busy making other plans."

John Lennon (1940 - 1980), English musician and singer-songwriter who rose to worldwide fame as one of the founding members of The Beatles, one of the most commercially successful and critically acclaimed acts in the history of popular music.

"Life isn't about finding yourself. Life is about creating yourself."

George Bernard Shaw (1856 - 1950), Irish writer and playwright who won the 1925 Nobel Prize for Literature.

"Life moves pretty fast. If you don't stop and look around once in a while, you could miss it."

Ferris Bueller (played by Matthew Broderick) in the movie *Ferris Bueller's Day Off* (1986).

"Life never seems the way we want it. But we must live it the best we can. There's no such thing as a perfect life, only a life sprinkled with perfect moments."

Unknown

"Life tends to respond to our outlook, to shape itself to meet our expectations."

Rich DeVos (1926 -), American businessman, Co-Founder of Amway and owner of the Orlando Magic NBA basketball team.

"Life without you would be like a broken pencil...pointless."

Rowan Atkinson (1955-), English comedian, screenwriter, and actor.

"Life would be infinitely happier if we could only be born at the age of eighty and gradually approach eighteen."

Mark Twain, the pen name of Samuel Langhorne Clemens (1835 - 1910, American writer and humorist.

"Linchpin: people who invent, lead (regardless of title), connect others, make things happen, and create order out of chaos."

Seth Godin (1960 -), American entrepreneur, author and public speaker. Godin popularized the topic of permission marketing.

"Live with intention. Walk to the edge. Listen hard. Practice wellness. Play with abandon. Laugh. Choose with no regret. Appreciate your friends. Continue to learn. Do what you love. Live as if this is all there is."

Mary Anne Radmacher

"Live, Love, Learn."

Title of a Nora Eason poem.

"Logic will get you from A to B. Imagination will take you everywhere."

Albert Einstein (1879 - 1955), German-born American physicist who developed the theories of relativity and won the Nobel Prize for Physics in 1921.

"Looking back, may I be filled with gratitude; looking forward, may I be filled with hope; looking upward, may I be aware of strength; looking inward, may I find peace......."

Unknown

"Lord grant me the serenity to accept the things I cannot change, the courage to change the things I can, and the wisdom to know the difference."

Saint Francis of Assisi (~ 1181 - 1226), Italian Catholic friar, preacher and Founder of the Franciscan Order.

"Love life, engage in it, give it all you've got. Love it with a passion, because life truly does give back, many times over, what you put into it."

Maya Angelou (1928 -), American author and poet.

"Many men go fishing all of their lives without knowing that it is not fish they are after."

Henry David Thoreau (1817 - 1862), American writer, poet and philosopher.

"Monday is an awful way to spend 1/7th of your life."

Unknown

"My interest is in the future because I am going to spend the rest of my life there."

Charles F. Kettering (1876 - 1958), American inventor, engineer, businessman, and the holder of 140 patents.

"Never lie, steal, cheat or drink. But if you must, lie in the arms of the one you love; steal away from bad company; cheat death; and drink in the moments that take your breath away."

Will Smith in the movie "Hitch" (2005).

"Never look down to test the ground before taking your next step; only he who keeps his eye fixed on the far horizon will find his right road."

Dag Hammarskjold (1905 - 1961), Swedish diplomat, economist and Nobel Prize winner.

"No good deed goes unpunished."

Clare Boothe Luce (1903 - 1987), American playwright, editor, journalist, ambassador, socialite and US Congresswoman, representing the state of Connecticut.

"No one will remember what you said or what you did - they will only remember how you made them feel."

Unknown

"Nobody can go back and start a new beginning, but anyone can start today and make a new ending."

Maria Robinson

"Nobody made a greater mistake than he who did nothing because he could do only a little."

Edmund Burke (1729 - 1797), Irish statesman, author, orator, political theorist, and philosopher.

"None are so old as those who have outlived enthusiasm."

Henry David Thoreau (1817 - 1862), American writer, poet and philosopher.

"Nothing gives one person so much advantage over another as to remain always cool and unruffled under all circumstances."

Thomas Jefferson (1743 - 1826), 3rd US President (1801 - 1809) and the primary writer of the Declaration of Independence in 1776.

"Nothing is a waste of time if you use the experience wisely."

Auguste Rodin (1840 - 1917), French sculptor.

"On the Internet, nobody knows you're a dog."

Peter Steiner from a cartoon in *The New Yorker*, July 5, 1993.

"One day your life will flash before your eyes. Make sure it's worth watching."

Unknown

"One of life's best coping mechanisms is to know the difference between an inconvenience and a problem. If you break your neck, if you have nothing to eat, if your house is on fire, then you've got a problem. Everything else is an inconvenience. Life is inconvenient. Life is lumpy. A lump in the oatmeal, a lump in the throat and a lump in the breast are not the same kind of lump. One needs to learn the difference."

Robert Fulghum (1937 -), American author, painter, sculptor and former minister.

"Our lives are not determined by what happens to us, but how we react to what happens; not by what life brings to us, but by the attitude we bring to life. A positive attitude causes a chain reaction of positive thoughts, events and outcomes. It is a catalyst. . . a spark that creates extraordinary results."

Unknown

"Playing is the recipe to stay young!"

Unknown

"Pray as if everything depended on GOD, act as if everything depended on yourself!"

Unknown

"Progress has not followed a straight ascending line, but a spiral with rhythms of progress and retrogression, of evolution and dissolution."

Johann Wolfgang von Goethe (1749 - 1832), German writer, philosopher and scientist.

"Purpose is what gives life meaning."

C.H. Parkhurst

"Quality questions create a quality life. Successful people ask better questions, and as a result, they get better answers."

Anthony Robbins (1960 -), American self-help author and success coach. His books include "Unlimited Power: The New Science of Personal Achievement" and "Awaken the Giant Within."

"Rainbows are just to look at, not to really understand."

Unknown

"Regret for the things we did can be tempered by time; it is regret for the things we did not do that is inconsolable."

Sidney J. Harris (1917 - 1986), London-born American journalist for the *Chicago Daily News* and later the *Chicago Sun-Times*.

"Seven Sins: Wealth without work, pleasure without conscience, knowledge without character, commerce without morality, science without humanity, worship without sacrifice, politics without principle."

Mahatma Gandhi (1869 - 1948), a pre-eminent political and ideological leader of India during the Indian independence movement.

"Shooting a picture is recognizing an event and at the same instant and within a fraction of a second rigorously organizing the forms you see to express and give meaning to the event. It is a matter of putting your brain, your eye and your heart in the same line of sight. It is a way of life."

Henri Cartier-Bresson (1908 - 2004), French photographer considered to be the father of modern photojournalism.

"Simplicity is the ultimate sophistication."

Leonardo da Vinci (1452 - 1519), Italian architect, engineer, painter, sculptor, inventor and scientist.

"Slow down and enjoy life. It's not only the scenery you miss by going too fast - you also miss the sense of where you are going and why."

Eddie Cantor (1892 - 1964), American "illustrated song" performer, comedian, dancer, singer, actor and songwriter.

"Some days you are the bird and some days you are the statue."

Unknown

"Some days you're a bug, some days you're a windshield."

Price Cobb (1954 -), American auto racer.

"Some have the wisdom of old age and the energy of youth. Most have the wisdom of youth, and the energy of old age."

Unknown

"Some men see things as they are and say why. I dream things that never were and say why not."

Robert F. Kennedy (1925 - 1968), American politician, a Democratic senator from New York, and a noted civil rights activist. An icon of modern American liberalism and member of the Kennedy family, he was a younger brother of President John F. Kennedy and acted as one of his advisors during his presidency. From 1961 to 1964, he was the US Attorney General.

"Sometimes in life, you have to dare to follow your heart; and hope that your head nods in agreement sooner or later."

Kenny Ray Morgan

"Television is bubble gum for the eyes."

Frank Lloyd Wright (1867 - 1959), American architect, interior designer, writer and educator, who designed more than 1,000 projects, which resulted in more than 500 completed works.

"The aging process has you firmly in its grasp if you never get the urge to throw a snowball."

Doug Larson (1926 -), American syndicated newspaper columnist.

"The best things in life aren't things."

Art Buchwald (1925 - 2007), American humorist best known for his long-running column in The Washington Post.

"The best way to predict your future is to create it."

Peter F. Drucker (1909 - 2006), American writer and management consultant.

"The best years of your life are the ones in which you decide your problems are your own. You don't blame them on your mother, the ecology, or the President. You realize that you control your own destiny."

Albert Ellis

"The big secret in life is that there is no big secret. Whatever your goal, you can get there if you're willing to work."

Oprah Winfrey (1954 -), American television host, actress, producer, and philanthropist, best known for her self-titled, multi-award winning talk show, which has become the highest rated program of its kind in history. She has been ranked the richest African American of the 20th century, the greatest black philanthropist in American history, and was once the world's only black billionaire. She is also, according to some assessments, the most influential woman in the world.

"The choice is between hanging on to the past and ruing what's lost or bracing for the road ahead and profiting from it. And the decision is purely one's own and has to come from within!"

Unknown

"The cost of a thing is the amount of what I will call life which is required to be exchanged for it, immediately or in the long run."

Henry David Thoreau (1817 - 1862), American writer, poet and philosopher.

"The difference between school and life? In school, you're taught a lesson and then given a test. In life, you're given a test that teaches you a lesson."

Tom Bodett (1955 -), American author, voice actor and radio host. He is also the current spokesman for the hotel chain Motel 6, whose commercials end with the phrase, "We'll leave the light on for you."

"The early bird catches the worm, but the second mouse get's the cheese."

Jon Hammond

"The future belongs to those who believe in the beauty and power of their dreams."

Eleanor Roosevelt (1884 - 1962), 32nd US first lady (1933 - 1945), UN diplomat, humanitarian.

"The future doesn't just happen - it's shaped by decisions."

Paul Tagliabue (1940 -), American and former National Football League (NFL) commissioner.

"The future will be better tomorrow."

Dan Quayle (1947 -), American, 44th US Vice President under George Bush (1989 - 1993).

"The game of life is the game of boomerangs. Our thoughts, deeds and words return to us sooner or later with astounding accuracy."

Florence Scovel Shinn (1871 - 1940), American writer, artist and teacher.

"The greatest pleasure in life is doing what people say you cannot do."

Walter Bagehot (1826 - 1877), English businessman, essayist, and journalist who wrote extensively about literature, government, and economic affairs.

"The happiest excitement in life is to be convinced that one is fighting for all one is worth on behalf of some clearly seen and deeply felt good."

Ruth Benedict (1887 - 1948), American anthropologist, cultural relativist, and folklorist.

"The hardest thing to learn in life is which bridge to cross and which to burn."

David Russell

"The meaning of life is a life with meaning."

Unknown

"The most difficult thing is the decision to act, the rest is merely tenacity. The fears are paper tigers. You can do anything you decide to do. You can act to change and control your life; and the procedure, the process is its own reward."

Amelia Carhart (1897 - 1937), American aviation pioneer and author.

"The most important choice you make is what you choose to make important."

Michael Neill

"The most important thing in life is not what people think you are but what you know yourself to be."

Leo Buscaglia (1924 - 1998), American author, motivational speaker, and a professor in the Department of Special Education at the University of Southern California.

"The most important things in life aren't things."

Anthony D'Angelo

"The path to our destination is not always a straight one. We go down the wrong road, we get lost, we turn back. Maybe it doesn't matter which road we embark on. Maybe what matters is that we embark."

Barbara Hall (1946 -), Canadian lawyer, public servant and former politician.

"The person who makes a success of living is the one who sees his goal steadily and aims for it unswervingly. That is dedication."

Cecil B. DeMille (1881 - 1959), American film director and Academy Award-winning film producer in both silent and sound films.

"The pure and simple truth is rarely pure and never simple."

Oscar Wilde (1854 - 1900), Irish dramatist, novelist and poet.

"The purpose of life is not to be happy - but to matter, to be productive, to be useful, to have it make some difference that you have lived at all."

Leo Rosten (1908 - 1997), Russian-born (in an area now part of Poland), teacher and academic. He is best known as a humorist in the fields of scriptwriting, story writing, journalism and Yiddish lexicography.

"The purpose of life is not to be happy. It is to be useful, to be honorable, to be compassionate, to have it make some difference that you have lived and lived well."

Ralph Waldo Emerson (1803 - 1882), American writer and poet.

"The purpose of life is to discover your gift. The meaning of life is to give your gift away."

David Viscott (1938 - 1996), American psychiatrist, author, businessman, and media personality.

"The purpose of life is to live it, to taste experience to the utmost, to reach out eagerly and without fear for newer and richer experience."

Eleanor Roosevelt (1884 - 1962), 32nd US first lady (1933 - 1945), UN diplomat and humanitarian.

"The thing that is really hard, and really amazing, is giving up on being perfect and beginning the work of becoming yourself."

Anna Quindlen (1953 -), American author, journalist, and opinion columnist whose New York Times column, Public and Private, won the Pulitzer Prize for Commentary in 1992.

"The true harvest of my life is intangible - a little star dust caught, a portion of the rainbow I have clutched."

Henry David Thoreau (1817 - 1862), American writer, poet and philosopher.

"The voyage of discovery is not in seeking new landscapes but in having new eyes."

Marcel Proust (1871 - 1922), French novelist, critic, and essayist.

"The way we communicate with others and with ourselves ultimately determines the quality of our lives."

Anthony Robbins (1960 -), American self-help author and success coach. His books include "Unlimited Power: The New Science of Personal Achievement" and "Awaken the Giant Within."

"The young man knows the rules, but the old man knows the exceptions."

Oliver Wendell Holmes (1809 - 1894), American physician, poet, writer, humorist and Professor at Harvard.

"There are two ways to live your life. One is as though nothing is a miracle. The other is as though everything is a miracle."

Albert Einstein (1879 - 1955), German-born American physicist who developed the theories of relativity and won the Nobel Prize for Physics in 1921.

"There comes a point in your life when you realize who really matters, who never did, and who always will."

Unknown

"There is more treasure in books than in all the pirates' loot on Treasure Island . . and best of all, you can enjoy these riches every day of your life."

Walt Disney (1901 - 1966), American film producer, director, screenwriter, voice actor, animator, entrepreneur, entertainer, international icon, and philanthropist. Disney is famous for his influence in the field of entertainment during the 20th century. As the Co-Founder (with his brother Roy O. Disney) of Walt Disney Productions, Disney became one of the best-known motion picture producers in the world. The corporation he co-founded, now known as The Walt Disney Company, today has annual revenues of approximately $35 billion.

"There is no future in spending the present worrying about the past."

Unknown

"There is only one thing more painful than learning from experience and that is not learning from experience."

Archibald McLeish (1892 - 1982), American poet, writer, and the Librarian of Congress.

"Things are more like they are now than they ever were before."

Harry S. Truman, 33rd US President (1945 - 1953).

"Things turn out best for the people that make the best of the way things turn out."

John Wooden (1910 - 2010), American Hall of Fame basketball coach for UCLA who won a record 10 NCAA men's championships.

"Things which matter most must never be at the mercy of the things that matter least."

Johann Wolfgang von Goethe (1749 - 1832), German writer, philosopher and scientist.

"Think of life as a terminal illness, because, if you do, you will live it with joy and passion, as it ought to be lived."

Anna Quindlen (1953 -), American author, journalist, and opinion columnist whose New York Times column, Public and Private, won the Pulitzer Prize for Commentary in 1992.

"This is as true in everyday life as it is in battle: we are given one life and the decision is ours whether to wait for circumstances to make up our mind, or whether to act, and in acting, to live."

General Omar Bradley (1893 - 1981), one of the main American army field commanders in North Africa and Europe during World War II.

"To do for the world more than the world does for you."

Henry Ford (1863 - 1947), prominent American industrialist, the founder of the Ford Motor Company, and sponsor of the development of the assembly line technique of mass production.

"To live is the rarest thing in the world. Most people exist is all."

Oscar Wilde (1854 - 1900), Irish dramatist, novelist and poet.

"To love is to risk not being loved in return. To hope is to risk pain. To try is to risk failure, but risk must be taken because the greatest hazard in life is to risk nothing."

Unknown

"Twenty years from now you will be more disappointed by the things you didn't do than by the ones you did do. So throw off the bowlines. Sail away from the safe harbor. Catch the trade winds in your sails. Explore. Dream. Discover."

Mark Twain, the pen name of Samuel Langhorne Clemens (1835 – 1910), American writer and humorist.

"Two questions asked when life is complete: Have you found joy in your life? And have you given joy to others?"

Excerpt from the movie "The Bucket List."

"Two roads diverged in a wood, and I took the one less travelled by, and that has made all the difference."

Robert Frost (1874 - 1963), American poet.

"Two things are infinite: the universe and human stupidity; and I'm not sure about the universe."

Albert Einstein (1879 - 1955), German-born American physicist who developed the theories of relativity and won the Nobel Prize for Physics in 1921.

"Ultimately, it's up to each of us to choose how we will live our lives, hold ourselves to high standards, and continually evaluate what's inside the image we see in the mirror."

Eric Harvey

"Walking is man's best medicine."

Hippocrates (~ 460 BC - ~ 370 BC), Greek physician of the Age of Pericles (Classical Athens), and is considered one of the most outstanding figures in the history of medicine.

"We are all faced with a series of great opportunities brilliantly disguised as impossible situations."

Charles R. Swindoll (1934 -), American evangelical Christian pastor, author, educator and radio preacher.

"We can't do anything about the length of our life. But we can surely do something about its depth!!"

Unknown

"We cannot change the cards we are dealt, just how we play the hand."

Randy Pausch (1960 - 2008), American professor of computer science and human-computer interaction and design at Carnegie Mellon University.

"We judge ourselves by what we feel capable of doing, while others judge us by what we have already done."

Henry Wadsworth Longfellow (1807 - 1882), American writer and poet.

"We make a living by what we do get, but we make a life by what we give."

Sir Winston Churchill (1874 - 1965), British orator, author and Prime Minister during World War II.

"We shall have no better conditions in the future if we are satisfied with all those which we have at present."

Thomas Edison (1847 - 1931), American inventor and salesman.

"What does it profit a man if he gains the whole world and loses his own soul?"

Robert Fulghum (1937 -), American author, painter, sculptor and former minister.

"What happened yesterday is history. What happens tomorrow is a mystery. What we do today makes a difference - the precious present moment."

Nick Saban (1951 -), highly successful American football coach at several prominent universities.

"What is the meaning of life? To be happy and useful."

Tenzin Gyatso (1935 -), Tibetan Buddhist leader and the 14th Dalai Lama. He won the Nobel Peace Prize in 1989, and is also well known for his lifelong advocacy for Tibetans inside and outside Tibet.

"What the caterpillar calls the end of the world, the master calls a butterfly"

Richard Bach (1936 -), American writer widely known as the author of the hugely popular 1970s best-sellers "Jonathan Livingston Seagull," and "Illusions: The Adventures of a Reluctant Messiah."

"What would life be if we had no courage to attempt anything?"

Vincent van Gogh (1853 - 1890), Dutch painter.

"What you leave behind is not what is engraved in stone monuments, but what is woven into the lives of others."

Pericles (495 BC - 429 BC), prominent and influential Greek statesman, orator, and general of Athens.

"When I do good, I feel good; when I do bad, I feel bad, and that is my religion."

Abraham Lincoln (attributed) (1809 - 1865), 16th US President. His term of office was from 1861 to 1865 and included the American Civil War.

"When is the last time you did something for the first time?"

Unknown

"When it comes to retirement, 75 may become the new 65."

R. M. Schneiderman

"When it's time to die, let us not discover that we have never lived."

Henry David Thoreau (1817 - 1862), American writer, poet and philosopher.

"When nothing goes Right take Left."

Unknown

"When one door closes, another opens; but we often look so long and so regretfully upon the closed door that we do not see the one that has opened for us."

Alexander Graham Bell (1847 - 1922), US inventor and teacher. Credited with the invention of the telephone in 1875.

"When you get to the end of your rope, tie a knot and hang on."

Franklin D. Roosevelt (1882 - 1945), 32nd US President (1933 - 1945).

"With all its sham, drudgery, and broken dreams, it is still a beautiful world."

Max Ehrmann (1872 - 1945), American writer and attorney. From "Desiderata."

"You can't turn back the clock. But you can wind it up again."

Bonnie Prudden (1914 -), a leading American rock climber in the 1940s and 1950s, with 30 documented first ascents to her credit.

"You must become a meaningful specific rather than a wandering generality."

Zig Ziglar (1926 -), American author, salesman, and motivational speaker.

"You only go around once in this life, so why not live a life you love? Start now. Live now. Love now. Laugh now. Give full expression to who you really are. Go for that deferred dream whether it's a new career, a new love, a new sport, or making yourself wealthy. You were put on this earth to be the best YOU that you can be."

BJ Gallagher, American author and speaker.

"You win a few, you lose a few. Some get rained out. But you got to dress for all of them."

Leroy Robert "Satchel" Paige (1906 - 1983), pitcher for the Pittsburgh Crawfords and the Kansas City Monarchs of the Negro Leagues; Cleveland Indians, St. Louis Browns and Kansas City Athletics of MLB (1926-53, 1965), Hall of Fame (1971).

"When asked what he thought of Western Civilization: 'I think it would be a good idea.'"

Mahatma Gandhi (1869 - 1948), a pre-eminent political and ideological leader of India during the Indian independence movement.

"You can't always get what you want, but if you try sometimes, you might find, you get what you need."

Lyric from a *Rolling Stones* Song "You Can't Always Get What You Want."

love
relationships

cry emotions ending enemies feel happiness laughter lies life

marriage power single

smile women

"A great marriage is not when the 'perfect couple' comes together. It is when an imperfect couple learns to enjoy their differences."

Dave Meurer

"A soul mate is someone who has locks that fit our keys, and keys to fit our locks. When we feel safe enough to open the locks, our truest selves step out and we can be completely and honestly who we are; we can be loved for who we are and not for who we're pretending to be. Each unveils the best part of the other. No matter what else goes wrong around us, with that one person we're safe in our own paradise. Our soul mate is someone who shares our deepest longings, our sense of direction. When we're two balloons, and together our direction is up, chances are we've found the right person. Our soul mate is the one who makes life come to life."

Richard Bach (1936 -), American writer widely known as the author of the hugely popular 1970s best-sellers "Jonathan Livingston Seagull," and "Illusions: The Adventures of a Reluctant Messiah."

"Among those whom I like or admire, I can find no common denominator, but among those whom I love, I can: all of them make me laugh."

W. H. Auden (1907 - 1973), Anglo-American poet, born in England, later an American citizen. Regarded by many as one of the greatest writers of the 20th century.

"Assumptions are the termites of relationships."

Henry Winkler (1945 -), American actor.

"Don't cry because it's over, smile because it happened."

Dr. Seuss (1904 - 1991), the penname of Theodor Geisel, American writer and cartoonist most widely known for his children's books.

"I like being single. I'm always there when I need me."

Art Leo

"If a man tells a woman she's beautiful she'll overlook most of his other lies."

Unknown

"If you were going to die soon and had only one phone call you could make, who would you call and what would you say? And why are you waiting?"

Stephen Levine

"Love begins with a smile, grows with a kiss and ends with a tear."

Unknown

"Love comes to those who still hope even though they've been disappointed, to those who still believe even though they've been betrayed, to those who still love even though they've been hurt before."

Unknown

"Love does not consist in gazing at each other but in looking outward together in the same direction."

Antoine de Saint Exupéry (1900 - 1944), a French writer and aviator. He is best remembered for his novella "The Little Prince" ("Le Petit Prince").

"Love doesn't make the world go round, love is what makes the ride worthwhile."

Franklin P. Jones

"Love is an exploding cigar we willingly smoke."

Lynda Barry (1956 -), American cartoonist and author.

"Love is like a friendship caught on fire. In the beginning a flame, very pretty, often hot and fierce, but still only light and flickering. As love grows older, our hearts mature and our love becomes as coals, deep-burning and unquenchable."

Bruce Lee (1940 - 1973), American actor and martial arts expert.

"Love is not about who you live with... It's about who you can't live without."

Unknown

"Love is not just gazing at each other but looking together in the same direction."

Unknown

"Love wasn't put in your heart to stay. Love isn't love until you give it away."

Michael W. Smith (1957 -), American singer.

"May your love be filled with life and may your life be filled with love."

Old wedding toast.

"Men always want to be a woman's first love. Women have a more subtle instinct; what they like to be is a man's last romance."

Unknown

"People love others not for who they are but for how they make them feel."

Irwin Federman

"Perhaps they are not stars, but rather openings in heaven where the love of our lost ones pours through and shines down upon us to let us know they are happy."

Eskimo proverb.

"Relationships of trust depend on our willingness to look not only to our own interests, but also the interests of others."

Peter Farquharson

"The desire of love is to give. The desire of lust is to get."

Ed Cole

"The 'Inside-Out' approach to personal and interpersonal effectiveness means to start first with self; even more fundamentally, to start with the most inside part of self / with your paradigms, your character, and your motives. The inside-out approach says that private victories precede public victories, that making and keeping promises to ourselves recedes making and keeping promises to others. It says it is futile to put personality ahead of character, to try to improve relationships with others before improving ourselves."

Stephen R. Covey (1932 -), Professor and author best known for the best-selling book, "The Seven Habits of Highly Effective People."

"The quality of your life is the quality of your relationships."

Anthony Robbins (1960 -), American self-help author and success coach. His books include "Unlimited Power: The New Science of Personal Achievement" and "Awaken the Giant Within."

"There is great comfort and inspiration in the feeling of close human relationships and its bearing on our mutual fortunes - a powerful force, to overcome the 'tough breaks' which are certain to come to most of us from time to time."

Walt Disney (1901 - 1966), American film producer, director, screenwriter, voice actor, animator, entrepreneur, entertainer, international icon, and philanthropist. Disney is famous for his influence in the field of entertainment during the 20th century. As the Co-Founder (with his brother Roy O. Disney) of Walt Disney Productions, Disney became one of the best-known motion picture producers in the world. The corporation he co-founded, now known as The Walt Disney Company, today has annual revenues of approximately $35 billion.

"There is no feeling more comforting and consoling than knowing you are right next to the one you love."

Unknown

"To love is to admire with the heart; to admire is to love with the mind."

Theophile Gautier (1811 - 1872), French poet, dramatist, novelist, journalist, art critic and literary critic.

"To the world you may be just one person, but to one person you may be the world!"

Brandi Snyder

"True friends are those who really know you but love you anyway."

Edna Buchanan (1939 -), American journalist and author best known for her crime mystery novels.

"True love is like a pair of socks: you gotta have two and they've gotta match."

Unknown

"We are most alive when we're in love."

John Updike (1932 - 2009), American novelist, poet, short story writer, art critic, and literary critic.

"We like someone because. We love someone although."

Henri de Montherlant (1895 - 1972), French essayist, novelist and one of the leading French dramatists of the twentieth century.

"Well, it seems to me that the best relationships - the ones that last - are frequently the ones that are rooted in friendship. You know, one day you look at the person and you see something more than you did the night before. Like a switch has been flicked somewhere. And the person who was just a friend is... suddenly the only person you can ever imagine yourself with."

Gillian Anderson (1968 -), American actress who played Dana Sculley in the TV series "X Files."

"When the power of love overpowers the love of power, the world will know peace."

Jimi Hendrix (1942 - 1970), American guitarist and singer-songwriter widely considered to be the greatest electric guitarist in musical history.

"Words are the seeds of emotion. Forgiveness is the seed for relationships."

Unknown

"You are simply my best time. You are my sweetest laughter. You are my most peaceful sleep... and still you find new ways to love me. Always you will have my hand to hold. Always . . ."

Mary Anne Radmacher

"You can't stop loving or wanting to love because when it's right, it's the best thing in the world. When you're in a relationship and it's good, even if nothing else in your life is right, you feel like your whole world is complete."

Keith Sweat (1963 -), American R&B/soul singer-songwriter and producer.

"You learn to like someone when you find out what makes them laugh, but you can never truly love someone until you find out what makes them cry."

Unknown

"You never lose by loving. You always lose by holding back."

Barbara De Angelis, American researcher on relationships and personal growth.

achievement attitude confidence failure faith force hop human spirit multiplier

opportunity

optimism
pessimism
problem solver success

"A pessimist always sees difficulty in every opportunity while an optimist always sees opportunity in every difficulty."

Sir Winston Churchill (1874 - 1965), British orator, author and Prime Minister during World War II.

"A pessimist is never disappointed."

Jack Cleary

"A pessimist is one who makes difficulties of his opportunities and an optimist is one who makes opportunities of his difficulties."

Harry S. Truman, 33rd US President (1945 - 1953).

"A pessimist is somebody who complains about the noise when opportunity knocks."

Oscar Wilde (1854 - 1900), Irish dramatist, novelist and poet.

"A pessimist sees only the dark side of the clouds, and mopes; a philosopher sees both sides, and shrugs; an optimist doesn't see the clouds at all - he's walking on them."

Leonard Louis Levinson

"An optimist is a driver who thinks that empty space at the curb won't have a hydrant beside it."

Jules Renard (1864 - 1910), French writer.

"An optimist is someone who figures that if it walks like a duck and quacks like a duck, it's the bluebird of happiness."

Robert Brault

"Both optimists and pessimists contribute to our society. The optimist invents the airplane and the pessimist the parachute."

G. B. Stern, British novelist.

"Don't worry about the world coming to an end today. It's already tomorrow in Australia."

Charles Schulz (1922 - 2000), American cartoonist best known for his comic strip "Peanuts."

"Few things in the world are more powerful than a positive push. A smile. A world of optimism and hope. A 'you can do it' when things are tough."

Dick M. DeVos (1955 -), American businessman and Republican politician from Michigan. The son of billionaire Amway co-founder Richard DeVos, he served as CEO of the multi-level marketing consumer goods distribution company from 1993 - 2002.

"Great leaders are pragmatists who can deal with difficult realities but still have the optimism and courage to act."

Nitin Nohria, Indian-born 10th and the current dean of Harvard Business School.

"I don't think you lead by pessimism and cynicism. I think you lead by optimism and enthusiasm and energy."

Patricia Ireland (1945 -), American administrator and feminist. She served as president of the National Organization for Women, from 1991 to 2001 and published an autobiography, "What Women Want," in 1996.

"I'm a pessimist because of intelligence, but an optimist because of will."

Antonio Gramsci (1891 - 1937), Italian writer, politician, political theorist, linguist and philosopher. He was a founding member and onetime leader of the Communist Party of Italy and was imprisoned by Benito Mussolini's Fascist regime.

"In the long run the pessimist may be proved right, but the optimist has a better time on the trip."

Daniel L. Reardon

"It's better to have lived life as an optimist who was wrong than as a pessimist who was right."

Unknown

"Losers visualize the penalties of failure. Winners visualize the rewards of success."

William S. Gilbert (1836 - 1911), English dramatist, librettist, poet and illustrator best known for his fourteen comic operas produced in collaboration with the composer Sir Arthur Sullivan, of which the most famous include "H.M.S. Pinafore," "The Pirates of Penzance" and one of the most frequently performed works in the history of musical theatre, "The Mikado."

"Many an optimist has become rich by buying out a pessimist."

Robert G. Allen (1902 - 1963), American businessman and a Democratic member of the US House of Representatives from Pennsylvania.

"No man ever injured his eyesight by looking on the bright side of things."

Unknown

"No pessimist ever discovered the secret of the stars, or sailed to an uncharted land, or opened a new doorway for the human spirit."

Helen Keller (1880 - 1968), American author, political activist, and lecturer. She was the first deafblind person to earn a Bachelor of Arts degree. The story of how Keller's teacher, Anne Sullivan, broke through the isolation imposed by a near complete lack of language, allowing the girl to blossom as she learned to communicate, has become widely known through the dramatic depictions of the play and film "The Miracle Worker."

"One of the things I learned the hard way was that it doesn't pay to get discouraged. Keeping busy and making optimism a way of life can restore your faith in yourself."

Lucille Ball (1911 - 1989), American comedian, film, television, stage and radio actress, model, film and television executive, and star of sitcoms like" I Love Lucy."

"Optimism is the faith that leads to achievement. Nothing can be done without hope and confidence."

Helen Keller (1880 - 1968), American author, political activist, and lecturer. She was the first deafblind person to earn a Bachelor of Arts degree. The story of how Keller's teacher, Anne Sullivan, broke through the isolation imposed by a near complete lack of language, allowing the girl to blossom as she learned to communicate, has become widely known through the dramatic depictions of the play and film "The Miracle Worker."

"Perpetual optimism is a force multiplier."

Colin Powell (1937 -), former Army General and US Secretary of State (2001 – 2005).

"Pessimism never won any battle."

Dwight D. Eisenhower, General and 34th US President (1953 - 1961).

"Pessimist: one who, when he has the choice of two evils, chooses both."

Oscar Wilde (1854 - 1900), Irish dramatist, novelist and poet.

"Stick with the optimists. It's going to be tough enough even if they're right."

James Reston (1909 - 1995), Scottish journalist.

"The average pencil is seven inches long, with just a half-inch eraser - in case you thought optimism was dead."

Robert Brault

"The man who is a pessimist before forty-eight knows too much; if he is an optimist after it he knows too little."

Mark Twain, the pen name of Samuel Langhorne Clemens (1835 - 1910), American writer and humorist.

"The nice part about being a pessimist is that you are constantly being either proven right or pleasantly surprised."

George Will (1941 -), American newspaper columnist, journalist, author and Pulitzer Prize-winner best known for his conservative commentary on politics.

"The optimist proclaims that we live in the best of all possible worlds; and the pessimist fears this is true."

James Branch Cabell (1879 - 1958), American author of fantasy fiction.

"The optimist says, 'My cup runneth over, what a blessing.' The pessimist says, 'My cup runneth over, what a mess.'"

Unknown

"The optimist sees the rose and not its thorns; the pessimist stares at the thorns, oblivious to the rose."

Kahil Gibran (1883 - 1931), Lebanese-born American philosophical essayist, novelist and poet.

"The pessimist complains about the wind; the optimist expects it to change; the realist adjusts the sails."

William Arthur Ward (1921 - 1994), American writer of inspirational articles, poems and meditations.

"We can complain because the rose bushes have thorns, or rejoice because thorn bushes have roses."

Abraham Lincoln (1809 - 1865), 16th US President. His term of office was from 1861 to 1865 and included the American Civil War.

"When it's raining outside we can still smile to brighten someone's day! 'It's A Beautiful Day!'"

Bono (1960 -), Irish singer, musician, and humanitarian best known for being the main vocalist of the Dublin-based rock band U2.

"When you have vision it affects your attitude. Your attitude is optimistic rather than pessimistic."

Charles R. Swindoll (1934 -), American evangelical Christian pastor, author, educator and radio preacher.

achievement aim ambition charity commitment contentment
courage courtesy daring determination encouragement energy
excellence expectations

failure

faith fundamentals

goals hard work health humility imitation impossible innovation integrity
laugh leap life lived losers love luck materialism money
obstacles opportunity outcome overnight passion
perserverance perseverence pleasing rich

success

value wealth wealthy winners wisdom
work

"A fine is a tax for doing wrong. A tax is a fine for doing well."

Unknown

"A man can fail many times, but he is not a failure until he begins to blame somebody else."

John Burroughs (1837 - 1921), American naturalist and essayist important in the evolution of the U.S. conservation movement.

"A word of encouragement during a failure is worth more than an hour of praise after success."

William Saroyan (1908 - 1981), Armenian American dramatist and author.

"Achievement seems to be connected with action. Successful men and women keep moving. They make mistakes, but they don't quit."

Conrad Hilton (1887 - 1979), American hotelier and founder of the Hilton Hotels chain.

"After all, success is not just an accident, it's the set of small 'success Habits' that allow to turn any dream to reality."

Unknown

"Being rich is having money, being wealthy is having time"

Margaret Bonnan

"Desire is the key to motivation, but it's the determination and commitment to an unrelenting pursuit of your goal -- a commitment to excellence --that will enable you to attain the success you seek."

Mario Andretti (1940 -), retired Italian-American world champion racing driver, one of the most successful Americans in the history of the sport.

"Difficult things take a long time, impossible things a little longer."

André A. Jackson

"Diligence is the mother of good luck."

Benjamin Franklin (1706 - 1790), American statesman, scientist, writer and printer.

"Don't fear failure so much that you refuse to try new things. The saddest summary of a life contains three descriptions: could have, might have, and should have."

Louis E. Boone (1941 -), American academic author.

"Failure is no more fatal than success is permanent."

Unknown

"Failure is not falling down, it is not getting up again."

Unknown

"Failure is simply the opportunity to begin again, this time more intelligently."

Henry Ford (1863 - 1947), prominent American industrialist, the founder of the Ford Motor Company, and sponsor of the development of the assembly line technique of mass production.

"Faith is taking the first step even when you don't see the whole staircase."

Martin Luther King Jr. (1929 - 1968), American civil rights leader and Nobel Peace Prize winner.

"For true success, it matters what our goals are. And it matters how we go about attaining them. The means are as important as the ends. How we get there is as important as where we go."

Tom Morris

"Great achievers do not necessarily do different things, they just do things differently."

Unknown

"He has achieved success who has lived well, laughed often, and loved much."

Bessie A. Stanley (before 1900 - 1952), American poet.

"I can accept failure; everyone fails at something. But I can't accept not trying."

Michael Jordan (1963 -), former American professional basketball player, active businessman, and majority owner of the Charlotte Bobcats. Considered the greatest basketball player of all time.

"I cannot give you the formula for success, but I can give you the formula for failure, which is: try to please everybody."

Herbert B. Swope (1882 - 1958), American editor and journalist considered by many to be the best reporter of his time.

"I'd rather do something and fail than do nothing and succeed!"

Unknown

"If one advances confidently in the direction of one's dreams, and endeavors to live the life which one has imagined, one will meet with a success unexpected in common hours."

Henry David Thoreau (1817 - 1862), American writer, poet and philosopher.

"If you really want to do something, you will find a way; if you do not, you will find an excuse."

Unknown

"If you want to feel rich, just count all of the things you have that money can't buy."

Robert Marlowe

"If you're not failing every now and again, it's a sign that you're not doing anything very innovative."

Woody Allen (1935 -), American screenwriter, director, actor, comedian, jazz musician, author, and playwright. Allen's distinctive films, which run the gamut from dramas to screwball sex comedies, have made him a notable American director.

"I'm a firm believer in luck, and I've found the harder I work, the luckier I get."

Thomas Jefferson (1743 - 1826), 3rd US President (1801 - 1809) and the primary writer of the Declaration of Independence in 1776.

"In order to succeed, you must know what you are doing, like what you are doing, and believe in what you are doing."

Will Rogers (1879 -1935) Cherokee-American cowboy, social commentator.

"In order to succeed, your desire for success MUST be greater than your fear of failure."

Bill Cosby (1937 -), American comedian, actor, author, television producer, educator, musician and activist.

"Instead of thinking about where you are, think about where you want to be. It takes twenty years of hard work to become an overnight success."

Diana Rankin

"It's good to have money and the things money can buy. But it's good, too, to check up once in a while and make sure you haven't lost the things money can't buy."

George Horace Lorimer (1867 - 1937), American journalist and author. He is best known as the editor of *The Saturday Evening Post*.

"It's better to fail in originality than to succeed in imitation."

Herman Melville (1819 - 1891), American novelist, short story writer, essayist, and poet best known for his novel "Moby Dick."

"I've always found that anything worth achieving will always have obstacles in the way and you've got to have that drive and determination to overcome those obstacles on route to whatever it is that you want to accomplish."

Chuck Norris (1940 -), American actor and martial artist.

"Look like a girl, act like a lady, think like a man and work like a dog."

Caroline K. Simon (1900 - 1993), American lawyer and politician.

"Many of life's failures are people who did not realize how close they were to success when they gave up."

Thomas Edison (1847 - 1931), American inventor and salesman.

"Materialism is buying things we don't need, with money we don't have, to impress people who don't matter."

Unknown

"No man ever achieved worthwhile success who did not, at one time or other, find himself with at least one foot hanging well over the brink of failure."

Napoleon Hill (1883 - 1970), American author.

"Nobody got anywhere in the world by simply being content."

Louis L'Amour (1908 - 1988), American author of primarily of Western fiction novels.

"Nothing splendid has ever been achieved except by those who dared believe that something inside themselves was superior to circumstance."

Bruce Barton (1886 - 1967), American advertising executive and US congressman.

"Opportunities always look bigger going than coming."

Unknown

"Opportunity is missed by most people because it is dressed in overalls and looks like work."

Thomas Edison (1847 - 1931), American inventor and salesman.

"Our greatest glory consists not in never falling, but in rising every time we fall."

Oliver Goldsmith (1730 - 1774), Irish-born British essayist, poet, novelist and dramatist.

"Patience and perseverance have a magical effect of making the difficulties disappear and obstacles vanish."

Thomaz Handy

"Patience, persistence and perspiration make an unbeatable combination for success."

Napoleon Hill (1883 - 1970), American author.

"People seldom see the halting and painful steps by which the most insignificant success is achieved."

Anne Sullivan (1866 - 1936), American teacher best known as the instructor and companion of Helen Keller.

"Remember that failure is an event - not a person."

Zig Ziglar (1926 -), American author, salesman, and motivational speaker.

"Six essential qualities that are the key to success: sincerity, personal integrity, humility, courtesy, wisdom, charity."

Dr. William Menninger (1899 - 1966), American Co-Founder (with his brother Karl and his father) of The Menninger Foundation in Topeka, Kansas, an internationally known center for treatment of behavioral disorders.

"Some succeed because they are destined to. But most succeed because they are determined to."

Henry Van Dyke (1852 - 1933), American short-story writer, poet and essayist.

"Strive for excellence. Success will follow you."

Unknown

"Strive not to be a success, but rather to be of value."

Albert Einstein (1879 - 1955), German-born American physicist who developed the theories of Relativity and won the Nobel Prize for Physics in 1921.

"Success does not depend on making important decisions quick, it depends on the quick action taken on important decisions."

Unknown

"Success happens when preparation meets opportunity."

Unknown

"Success has many fathers, failure is always a bastard."

Unknown

"Success is a journey, not a destination. The doing is often more important than the outcome."

Arthur Ashe (1943 - 1993), American professional tennis player.

"Success is almost totally dependent upon drive and persistence. The extra energy required to make another effort or try another approach is the secret of winning."

Denis Waitley (1933 -), American motivational speaker and writer, consultant and best-selling author.

"Success is doing ordinary things extraordinarily well."

Jim Rohn (1930 - 2009), American entrepreneur, author and motivational speaker. His rags to riches story played a large part in his work, which influenced others in the personal development industry.

"Success is focusing the full power of all you are on what you have a burning desire to achieve."

Wilfred Oeterson

"Success is largely a matter of holding on after others have let go."

Unknown

"Success is neither magical nor mysterious. Success is the natural consequence of consistently applying the basic fundamentals."

Jim Rohn (1930 - 2009), American entrepreneur, author and motivational speaker. His rags to riches story played a large part in his work, which influenced others in the personal development industry.

"Success is not final, failure is not fatal; it is the courage to continue that counts."

Sir Winston Churchill (1874 - 1965), British orator, author and Prime Minister during World War II.

"Success is not the key to happiness. Happiness is the key to success. If you love what you are doing, you will be successful."

Albert Schweitzer (1875 - 1965), Franco-German (Alsatian) theologian, organist, philosopher, physician, and medical missionary.

"Success is not the result of spontaneous combustion. You must set yourself on fire."

Reggie Leach (1950 -), retired Canadian professional ice hockey right winger who played 13 seasons in the National Hockey League (NHL).

"Success is not to be sought after, it eventually gets attracted to the person who you become."

Jim Rohn (1930 - 2009), American entrepreneur, author and motivational speaker. His rags to riches story played a large part in his work, which influenced others in the personal development industry.

"Success is peace of mind which is a direct result of self-satisfaction in knowing you did your best to become the best you are capable of becoming."

John Wooden (1910 - 2010), American Hall of Fame basketball coach for UCLA who won a record 10 NCAA men's championships.

"Success is simple. Do what's right, the right way, at the right time."

Arnold Glasow

"Success is that old ABC - ability, breaks and courage."

Charles Luckman (1909 - 1999), American businessman and architect.

"Success is the ability to go from one failure to another with no loss of enthusiasm."

Sir Winston Churchill (1874 - 1965), British orator, author and Prime Minister during World War II.

"Success is the maximum utilization of the ability that you have."

Zig Ziglar (1926 -), American author, salesman, and motivational speaker.

"Success is to be measured not so much by the position that one has reached in life as by the obstacles which one has overcome while trying to succeed."

Booker T. Washington (1856 - 1915), American educator and political activist.

"Success often lies just a few steps beyond the point where you decide to quit."

Unknown

"Success on any major scale requires you to accept responsibility... in the final analysis, the one quality that all successful people have... is the ability to take on responsibility."

Michael Korda (1933 -), British writer and novelist who was editor-in-Chief of Simon & Schuster in New York City.

"Success usually comes to those who are too busy to be looking for it."

Henry David Thoreau (1817 - 1862), American writer, poet and philosopher.

"The definition of luck is when opportunity meets preparation."

Unknown

"The elevator to success is out of order. You'll have to use the stairs, one step at a time."

Joe Girard (1928 -), American salesman. He is recognized by the Guinness Book of World Records as the world's greatest salesman for twelve consecutive years, selling 13,001 cars at a Chevrolet dealership between 1963 and 1978.

"The greatest danger for most of us is not that our aim is too high and we miss it, but that it is too low and we reach it."

Michelangelo (1475 - 1564), Italian sculptor, painter, poet and architect of the Renaissance.

"The only place where success comes before work is a dictionary."

Vidal Sassoon (1928 -), a British hairdresser and businessman.

"The person who gets the farthest is generally the one who is willing to do and dare. The sure-thing boat never gets far from shore."

Dale Carnegie (1888 - 1955), American writer, lecturer, and the developer of famous courses in self-improvement, salesmanship, corporate training, public speaking, and interpersonal skills. He's best known as author of "How to Win Friends and Influence People" (1936).

"The price of success is hard work, dedication to the job at hand, and the determination that whether we win or lose, we have applied the best of ourselves to the task at hand."

Vince Lombardi (1913 - 1970), American football coach best known as the head coach of the Green Bay Packers during the 1960s.

"The probability that we may fail in the struggle ought not to deter us from the support of a cause we believe to be just."

Abraham Lincoln (1809 - 1865), 16th US President. His term of office was from 1861 to 1865 and included the American Civil War.

"The quickest way to double your money is to fold it over and put it back in your pocket."

Will Rogers (1879 -1935) Cherokee-American cowboy, social commentator.

"The road to success is always under construction."

Lily Tomlin (1939 -), American actress and comedian.

"The road to success is dotted with many tempting parking places."

Unknown

"There are no secrets to success. It is the result of preparation, hard work, learning from failure."

Colin Powell (1937 -), former Army General and US Secretary of State (2001 – 2005).

"There's always a way - if you're committed."

Anthony Robbins (1960 -), American self-help author and success coach. His books include "Unlimited Power: The New Science of Personal Achievement" and "Awaken the Giant Within."

"To laugh often and love much; to win the respect of intelligent persons and the affection of children; to earn the approbation of honest citizens and endure the betrayal of false friends; to appreciate beauty; to find the best in others; to give of one's self; to leave the world a bit better, whether by a healthy child, a garden patch or a redeemed social condition; to have played and laughed with enthusiasm and sung with exultation; to know even one life has breathed easier because you have lived - this is to have succeeded."

Ralph Waldo Emerson (1803 - 1882), American writer and poet.

"To succeed you need to find something to hold on to, something to motivate you, something to inspire you."

Tony Dorsett (1954 -), former American football running back in the National Football League (NFL) for the Dallas Cowboys and Denver Broncos.

"We must walk consciously only part way toward our goal, and then leap in the dark to our success."

Henry David Thoreau (1817 - 1862), American writer, poet and philosopher.

"What separates the winners from the losers is how a person reacts to each new twist of fate."

Donald Trump (1946 -), American business magnate, socialite, author, and television personality.

"We spend our entire lives sacrificing our health for our wealth and then when we get to retirement we sacrifice all of our wealth to regain our health."

A.J. Reb Materi

"What would you attempt to do if you knew you could not fail?"

Robert Schuller (1926 -), American televangelist, pastor, and author known principally through the weekly "Hour of Power" television broadcast that he began in 1970.

"Whatever women do they must do twice as well as men to be thought half as good. Luckily this is not difficult."

Charlotte Whitton (1896 - 1975), Canadian feminist and Mayor of Ottawa.

"Where the heart is willing it will find a thousand ways, but where it is unwilling it will find a thousand excuses."

Dayak proverb.

"Why not go out on a limb? That's where the fruit is."

Mark Twain, the pen name of Samuel Langhorne Clemens (1835 - 1910), American writer and humorist.

"You can have everything in life you want, if you will just help other people get what they want."

Zig Ziglar (1926 -), American author, salesman, and motivational speaker.

"You can only become truly accomplished at something you love. Don't make money your goal. Instead, pursue the things you love doing, and then do them so well that people can't take their eyes off you."

Maya Angelou (1928 -), American author and poet.

"You always pass failure on your way to success."

Mickey Rooney (1920 -), American film actor and entertainer whose film, television, and stage appearances span nearly his entire lifetime.

"You have to see the opportunity before it become obvious."

Peter F. Drucker (1909 - 2006), American writer and management consultant.

"You may have a fresh start any moment you choose, for this thing that we call 'failure' is not the falling down, but the staying down."

Mary Pickford (1892 - 1979), Canadian actress and Co-Founder of United Artists.

"Your success in life will be in direct proportion to what you do after you do what you are expected to do."

Unknown, quoted in the book "Goals" by Brian Tracy.

"You've achieved success in your field when you don't know whether what you're doing is work or play."

Warren Beatty (1937 -), American actor, producer, screenwriter and director. He has received a total of ten Academy Award nominations, winning one for Best Director in 1982.

action   clock   courage   dogma   future   money   present   purpose   quality

time value

"Children spell love... T-I-M-E."

Dr. Anthony P. Witham

"Don't let the fear of the time it will take to accomplish something stand in the way of your doing it. The time will pass anyway; we might just as well put that passing time to the best possible use."

Earl Nightingale (1921 - 1989), American motivational speaker and author, known as the "Dean of Personal Development."

"Don't count every hour in the day, make every hour in the day count."

Alfred Binet (1857 - 1911), French psychologist and inventor of the first usable intelligence test, known at that time as the Binet test and today basically referred to as an IQ test.

"Don't say you don't have enough time. You have exactly the same number of hours per day that were given to Helen Keller, Pasteur, Michelangelo, Mother Teresa, Leonardo da Vinci, Thomas Jefferson, and Albert Einstein."

H. Jackson Brown, Jr., American best selling writer and author of "Life's Little Instruction Book."

"How did it get so late so soon?"

Dr. Seuss (1904 - 1991), the penname of Theodor Geisel, American writer and cartoonist most widely known for his children's books.

"I cannot promise very much. I give you the images I know. Lie still with me and watch. We laugh and we touch. I promise you love. Time will not take that away."

Anne Sexton (1928 - 1974), influential American poet, known for her highly personal, confessional verse. She won the Pulitzer Prize for poetry in 1967.

"It's only when we truly know and understand that we have a limited time on earth - and that we have no way of knowing when our time is up, we will then begin to live each day to the fullest, as if it was the only one we had."

Elisabeth Kubler-Ross (1926 - 2004), Swiss-born psychiatrist, a pioneer in near-death studies and the author of the groundbreaking book "On Death and Dying" (1969).

"Lost time is never found again."

Benjamin Franklin (1706 - 1790), American statesman, scientist, writer and printer.

"Our time is limited, so don't waste it living someone else's life. Don't be trapped by dogma — which is living with the results of other people's thinking. Don't let the noise of others' opinions drown out your own inner voice. And most important, have the courage to follow your heart and intuition. They somehow already know what you truly want to become. Everything else is secondary."

Steve Jobs (1955 -), American businessman and Co-Founder at Apple Inc., the inventor of Mac computers, iPods, iPhones and iPads.

"The best thing about the future is that it comes one day at a time."

Abraham Lincoln (1809 - 1865), 16th US President. His term of office was from 1861 to 1865 and included the American Civil War.

"The problem with the future is it turns into the present."

Unknown

"The secret of life is enjoying the passage of time."

James Taylor (1948 -), American singer-songwriter and guitarist inducted into the Rock & Roll Hall of Fame in 2000. Taylor achieved his major breakthrough in 1970 with "Fire and Rain" and had his first #1 hit the following year with "You've Got a Friend", a recording of Carole King's classic song.

"The time is always right to do what is right."

Martin Luther King Jr. (1929 - 1968), American civil rights leader and Nobel Peace Prize winner.

"The time to take time is when there is no time."

Unknown

"The time you enjoy wasting is not wasted time."

Bertrand Russell (1872 - 1970), English logician and philosopher.

"There is never time to do it right but always time to do it over."

Unknown

"This time, like all times, is a very good one, if we but know what to do with it."

Ralph Waldo Emerson (1803 - 1882), American writer and poet.

"Time and money spent in helping men do more for themselves is far better than mere giving."

Henry Ford (1863 - 1947), prominent American industrialist, the founder of the Ford Motor Company, and sponsor of the development of the assembly line technique of mass production.

"Time discovers truth."

Seneca (~ 54 BC - ~ 39 AD), Roman rhetorician and writer.

"Time goes by so fast, people go in and out of your life. You must never miss the opportunity to tell these people how much they mean to you."

Unknown

"Time has a wonderful way of showing us what really matters."

Margaret Peters

"Time is a circus, always packing up and moving away."

Ben Hecht (1893 - 1964), American film writer, novelist, playwright and newspaperman.

"Time is a sort of river of passing events, and strong is its current; no sooner is a thing brought to sight than it is swept by and another takes its place, and this too will be swept away."

Marcus Aurelius (~ 121 AD - 180 AD), Roman Emperor (161 AD - 180 AD) and philosopher.

"Time is at once the most valuable and the most perishable of all our possessions."

John Randolph

"Time is free, but it's priceless. You can't own it, but you can use it. You can't keep it, but you can spend it. Once you've lost it you can never get it back."

Harvey MacKay (1932 -), American businessman, columnist and author.

"Time is like money: you can either spend, waste, or invest!"

Unknown

"Time is limited, so I better wake up every morning fresh and know that I have just one chance to live this particular day right, and to string my days together into a life of action and purpose."

Lance Armstrong (1971 -), American cyclist, 7-time winner of the Tour de France, cancer survivor.

"Time is relative... The mind makes it slow, the heart makes it fast, our friends make it worthwhile, and words... make it timeless."

Unknown

"Time is the most precious element of human existence. The successful person knows how to put energy into time and how to draw success from time."

Denis Waitley (1933 -), American motivational speaker and writer, consultant and best-selling author.

"Time is the scarcest resource and unless it is managed nothing else can be managed."

Peter F. Drucker (1909 - 2006), American writer and management consultant.

"Time is too slow for those who wait, too swift for those who fear, too long for those who grieve, too short for those who rejoice, but for those who love, time is eternity."

Henry Van Dyke (1852 - 1933), American short-story writer, poet and essayist.

"Time is what we want most, but what we use worst."

William Penn (1644 - 1718), English real estate entrepreneur, philosopher, and founder and "absolute proprietor" of the Province of Pennsylvania, the English North American colony and the future Commonwealth of Pennsylvania. He was an early champion of democracy and religious freedom, notable for his good relations and successful treaties with the Lenape Indians. Under his direction, the city of Philadelphia was planned and developed.

"To achieve great things, two things are needed; a plan, and not quite enough time."

Leonard Bernstein (1918 - 1990), American conductor, composer and pianist.

"Today is the tomorrow you worried about yesterday."

Unknown

"Today is tomorrow's yesterday...make the best of it... for it will never come again."

Janice Markowitz

"Today is yesterday's effect and tomorrow's cause."

Phillip Gribble

"Until you value yourself, you will not value your time. Until you value your time, you will not do anything with it."

M. Scott Peck (1936 - 2005), American psychiatrist and best-selling author, best known for his first book, "The Road Less Traveled" (1978).

"We all have our time machines. Some take us back, they're called memories. Some take us forward, they're called dreams."

Jeremy Irons (1948 -), English actor on stage, in movies and on television.

"We always have time enough, if we but use it right."

Johann Wolfgang von Goethe (1749 - 1832), German writer, philosopher and scientist.

"Yesterday is a canceled check; tomorrow is a promissory note; today is the only cash you have - so spend it wisely."

Kay Lyons

"You can't have a better tomorrow if you are thinking about yesterday all the time."

Charles F. Kettering (1876 - 1958), American inventor, engineer, businessman, and the holder of 140 patents.

Quotations by Sir Winston Churchill (1874 - 1965), British orator, author and Prime Minister during World War II:

action / goals / initiative	"Continuous effort - not strength or intelligence - is the key to unlocking our potential."
attitude	"A man is about as big as the things that make him angry."
attitude	"Attitude is a little thing that makes a big difference."
attitude	"Courage is what it takes to stand up and speak. Courage is also what it takes to sit down and listen."
attitude	"It's not enough that we do our best; sometimes we have to do what's required."
attitude	"Kites rise highest against the wind, not with it."
attitude	"Never give in, never give in, never; never; never; never - in nothing, great or small, large or petty - never give in except to convictions of honor and good sense."

attitude	"Sometimes doing your best is not good enough. Sometimes you must do what is required."
attitude	"The first quality that is needed is audacity."
attitude	"The truth is incontrovertible, malice may attack it, ignorance may deride it, but in the end; there it is."
attitude	"True genius resides in the capacity for evaluation of uncertain, hazardous, and conflicting opinions."
friends / enemies	"You have enemies? Good. That means you've stood up for something, sometime in your life."
government / politics	"I contend that for a nation to try to tax itself into prosperity is like a man standing in a bucket and trying to lift himself up by the handle."
government / politics	"It has been said that democracy is the worst form of government except all the others that have been tried."
government / politics	"The best argument against democracy is a five-minute conversation with the average voter."

government / politics	"When I am abroad, I always make it a rule to never criticize or attack the government of my own country. I make up for lost time when I come home."
government / politics	"You can always count on the American people to do the right thing. Once they have exhausted all of the alternatives."
humor	"I like pigs better than cat and dogs. Dogs are subservient and look up to man. Cats are aloof and look down on man. A pig, however, will look you in the eye, and see his equal."
leadership	"Before you can inspire with emotion, you must be swamped with it yourself. Before you can move their tears, your own must flow. To convince them, you must yourself believe."
leadership	"The inherent vice of capitalism is the unequal sharing of the blessings. The inherent blessing of socialism is the equal sharing of misery."
leadership	"When you have an important point to make, don't try to be subtle or clever. Use a pile driver. Hit the point once. Then come back and hit it again. Then hit it a third time - a tremendous whack."
learning / knowledge / wisdom	"My education was interrupted only by my schooling."

life	"All the great things are simple, and many can be expressed in a single word: freedom; justice; honor; duty; mercy; hope."
life	"History is written by the victors."
life	"If you are going through hell - keep going."
life	"We make a living by what we do get, but we make a life by what we give."
optimism / pessimism	"A pessimist always sees difficulty in every opportunity while an optimist always sees opportunity in every difficulty."
success / failure	"Success is not final, failure is not fatal; it is the courage to continue that counts."
success / failure	"Success is the ability to go from one failure to another with no loss of enthusiasm."

Quotations by Albert Einstein (1879 - 1955), German-born American physicist who developed the theories of relativity and won the Nobel Prize for Physics in 1921:

attitude   **"Be profound, be funny, or be quiet!!"**

attitude   **"Common sense is the collection of prejudices acquired by age eighteen."**

attitude   **"Great spirits have always encountered violent opposition from mediocre minds."**

attitude   **"Insanity is doing the same thing over again and expecting different results."**

attitude   **"It is a miracle curiosity survives formal education."**

attitude   **"The Three Rules of Work: 1. Out of clutter, find simplicity. 2. From discord, find harmony. 3. In the middle of difficulty lies opportunity."**

attitude   **"Unthinking respect for authority is the greatest enemy of truth."**

character	"Most people say that is it is the intellect which makes a great scientist. They are wrong: it is character."
character	"Try not to become a man of success, but rather try to become a man of value."
learning / knowledge / wisdom	"I never teach my pupils; I only attempt to provide the conditions in which they can learn."
learning / knowledge / wisdom	"If you can't explain it simply, you don't understand it well enough."
learning / knowledge / wisdom	"Imagination is more important than knowledge. For knowledge is limited to all we now know and understand, while imagination embraces the entire world, and all there ever will be to know and understand."
learning / knowledge / wisdom	"It is the supreme art of the teacher to awaken joy in creative expression and knowledge."
learning / knowledge / wisdom	"The difference between stupidity and genius is that genius has its limits."
learning / knowledge / wisdom	"The level of thinking that got us here is going to have to be exceeded to get us out of here."

learning / knowledge / wisdom	**"We can't solve problems by using the same kind of thinking we used when we created them."**
life	**"Imagination is everything. It is the preview of life's coming attractions."**
life	**"Learn from yesterday, live for today, hope for tomorrow. The important thing is not to stop questioning."**
life	**"Logic will get you from A to B. Imagination will take you everywhere."**
life	**"There are two ways to live your life. One is as though nothing is a miracle. The other is as though everything is a miracle."**
life	**"Two things are infinite: the universe and human stupidity; and I'm not sure about the universe."**
success / failure	**"Strive not to be a success, but rather to be of value."**

Quotations by Ralph Waldo Emerson (1803 - 1882), American writer and poet:

action / initiative	**"To map out a course of action and follow it to an end requires courage."**
attitude	**"Nothing great was ever achieved without enthusiasm."**
attitude	**"The only person you are destined to become is the person you decide to be."**
attitude	**"What lies before us and what lies behind us are tiny matters compared to what lies within us."**
attitude	**"Whatever course you decide upon, there is always someone to tell you that you are wrong. There are always difficulties arising which tempt you to believe that your critics are right. To map out a course of action and follow it to an end requires courage."**
attitude	**"Wise men put their trust in ideas and not in circumstances."**
character	**"People do not seem to realize that their opinion of the world is also a confession of character."**
life	**"Do not go where the path may lead go instead where there is no path and leave a trail."**
life	**"It is not length of life, but depth of life."**

life

"Life is a succession of lessons, which must be lived to be understood."

life

"The purpose of life is not to be happy. It is to be useful, to be honorable, to be compassionate, to have it make some difference that you have lived and lived well."

success / failure

"To laugh often and love much; to win the respect of intelligent persons and the affection of children; to earn the approbation of honest citizens and endure the betrayal of false friends; to appreciate beauty; to find the best in others; to give of one's self; to leave the world a bit better, whether by a healthy child, a garden patch or a redeemed social condition; to have played and laughed with enthusiasm and sung with exultation; to know even one life has breathed easier because you have lived - this is to have succeeded."

time

"This time, like all times, is a very good one, if we but know what to do with it."

Quotations by Robert Fulghum (1937 -), American author, painter, sculptor and former minister:

action / goals / initiative	"The world does not need tourists who ride by in a bus clucking their tongues. The world as it is needs those who will love it enough to change it, with what they have, where they are."
attitude	"He who laughs, lasts."
children / family / parenting	"Don't worry that children never listen to you; worry that they are always watching you."
government / politics	"It'll be a great day when education gets all the money it wants and the Air Force has to hold a bake sale to buy bombers."
learning / knowledge / wisdom	"All I really need to know about how to live and what to do and how to be I learned in kindergarten. Remember the Dick-and-Jane books and the first word you learned -- the biggest word of all -- look."
life	"Be aware of wonder. Live a balanced life - learn some and think some and draw and paint and sing and dance and play and work every day some."
life	"I believe that imagination is stronger than knowledge - myth is more potent than history - dreams are more powerful than facts - hope always triumphs over experience - laughter is the cure for grief - love is stronger than death."

life   "I've always thought anyone can make money.
                                  Making a life worth living, that's the real test."

life   "One of life's best coping mechanisms is to
                                  know the difference between an inconvenience
                                  and a problem. If you break your neck, if you
                                  have nothing to eat, if your house is on fire,
                                  then you've got a problem. Everything else is an
                                  inconvenience. Life is inconvenient. Life is
                                  lumpy. A lump in the oatmeal, a lump in the
                                  throat and a lump in the breast are not the
                                  same kind of lump. One needs to learn the
                                  difference."

life   "What does it profit a man if he gains the whole
                                  world and loses his own soul?"

Quotations by Anthony Robbins (1960 -), American self-help author and success coach. His books include "Unlimited Power: The New Science of Personal Achievement" and "Awaken the Giant Within."

action / goals / initiative   **"Put yourself in a state of mind where you can say to yourself, "Here is an opportunity for you to celebrate like never before, my own power, my own ability to get myself to do whatever is necessary."**

attitude   **"I believe that the level of success we experience in life is in direct proportion to the level of our commitment to CANI!, to Constant and Never-Ending Improvement."**

attitude   **"Live with passion!"**

attitude   **"We usually overestimate what we think we can accomplish in one year; but we grossly underestimate what we can accomplish in a decade."**

attitude   **"You are now at a crossroads. This is your opportunity to make the most important decision you will ever make. Forget your past. Who are you now? Who have you decided you really are now? Don't think about who you have been. Who are you now? Who have you decided to become? Make this decision consciously. Make it carefully. Make it powerfully."**

life	"If you don't set a baseline standard for what you'll accept in life, you'll find it's easy to slip into behaviors and attitudes or a quality of life that's far below what you deserve."
life	"It is not what we get. But who we become, what we contribute... that gives meaning to our lives."
life	"Quality questions create a quality life. Successful people ask better questions, and as a result, they get better answers."
life	"The way we communicate with others and with ourselves ultimately determines the quality of our lives."
love / relationships	"The quality of your life is the quality of your relationships."
success / failure	"There's always a way - if you're committed."

Quotations by Jim Rohn (1930 - 2009), American entrepreneur, author and motivational speaker. His rags to riches story played a large part in his work, which influenced others in the personal development industry.

action / goals / initiative	**"Goals. There's no telling what you can do when you get inspired by them. There's no telling what you can do when you believe in them. There's no telling what will happen when you act upon them."**
action / goals / initiative	**"Motivation is what gets you started. Habit is what keeps you going."**
action / goals / initiative	**"The ultimate reason for setting goals is to entice you to become the person it takes to achieve them."**
attitude	**"Discipline is the bridge between goals and accomplishments."**
attitude	**"Let others lead small lives, but not you. Let others argue over small things, but not you. Let others cry over small hurts, but not you. Let others leave their future in someone else's hands, but not you."**
attitude	**"When you know what you want, and want it bad enough, you will find a way to get it."**
attitude	**"You cannot change your destination overnight, but you can change your direction overnight."**
attitude	**"You don't get paid for the hour. You get paid for the value you bring to the hour."**

change	"I find it fascinating that most people plan their vacations with better care than they plan their lives. Perhaps that is because escape is easier than change."
success / failure	"Success is doing ordinary things extraordinarily well."
success / failure	"Success is neither magical nor mysterious. Success is the natural consequence of consistently applying the basic fundamentals."
success / failure	"Success is not to be sought after, it eventually gets attracted to the person who you become."

Quotations by Eleanor Roosevelt (1884 - 1962), 32nd US first lady (1933 - 1945), UN diplomat, and humanitarian:

attitude	**"Believe in yourself. You gain strength, courage, and confidence by every experience in which you stop to look fear in the face. . . You must do that which you think you cannot do."**
attitude	**"Great minds discuss ideas; average minds discuss events; small minds discuss people."**
attitude	**"I think that somehow, we learn who we really are and then live with that decision."**
attitude	**"No one can make you feel inferior without your consent."**
attitude	**"We gain strength, and courage, and confidence by each experience in which we really stop to look fear in the face... we must do that which we think we cannot."**
change	**"Do one thing every day that scares you."**
character	**"People grow through experience if they meet life honestly and courageously. This is how character is built."**

friends / enemies	"Many people will walk in and out of your life, but only true friends will leave footprints in your heart."
leadership	"Never let anyone tell you no who doesn't have the power to say yes."
learning / knowledge / wisdom	"Learn from the mistakes of others. You can't live long enough to make them all yourself."
life	"The future belongs to those who believe in the beauty and power of their dreams."
life	"The purpose of life is to live it, to taste experience to the utmost, to reach out eagerly and without fear for newer and richer experience."

Quotations by Theodore Roosevelt (1858 - 1919), 26th US President (1901 - 1909):

action / goals / initiative   **"Far and away the best prize that life offers is the chance to work hard at work worth doing."**

attitude   **"Whenever you are asked if you can do a job, tell 'em, 'Certainly, I can!' Then get busy and find out how to do it."**

character   **"Character, in the long run, is the decisive factor in the life of an individual and of nations alike."**

character   **"I care not what others think of what I do, but I care very much about what I think of what I do. That is character!"**

government / politics   **"A typical vice of American politics is the avoidance of saying anything real on real issues."**

government / politics   **"When they call the roll in the Senate, the Senators do not know whether to answer 'Present' or 'Not guilty.'"**

leadership

"Far better it is to dare mighty things, to win glorious triumphs even though checkered by failure, than to rank with those timid spirits who neither enjoy nor suffer much because they live in the gray twilight that knows neither victory nor defeat."

leadership

"In any moment of decision, the best thing you can do is the right thing. The next best thing you can do is the wrong thing. The worst thing you can do is nothing."

leadership

"It is not the critic who counts; not the man who points out how the strong man stumbles, or where the doer of deeds could have done them better. The credit belongs to the man who is actually in the arena, whose face is marred by dust and sweat and blood, who strives valiantly; who errs and comes short again and again; because there is not effort without error and shortcomings; but who does actually strive to do the deed; who knows the great enthusiasm, the great devotion, who spends himself in a worthy cause, who at the best knows in the end the triumph of high achievement and who at the worst, if he fails, at least he fails while daring greatly. So that his place shall never be with those cold and timid souls who know neither victory nor defeat."

leadership

"The best leader is the one who has sense enough to pick good men to do what he wants done, and self-restraint enough to keep from meddling with them while they do it."

Quotations by George Bernard Shaw (1856 - 1950), Irish writer and playwright who won the 1925 Nobel Prize for Literature:

attitude   "People are always blaming their circumstances for what they are. I don't believe in circumstances. The people who get on in this world are the people who get up and look for the circumstances they want, and if they can't find them, they make them."

attitude   "The power of accurate observation is commonly called cynicism by those who have not got it."

attitude   "The reasonable man adapts himself to the world; the unreasonable one persists in trying to adapt the world to himself. Therefore all progress depends on the unreasonable man."

attitude   "The single biggest problem in communication is the illusion that it has taken place."

attitude   "We don't stop playing because we grow old; we grow old because we stop playing."

attitude   "You see things and you say, 'Why?' but I dream things that never were and I say 'Why not?'"

government / politics	"A government which robs Peter to pay Paul can always depend on the support of Paul."
happiness	"You can easily find people who are ten times as rich at sixty as they were at twenty; but not one of them will tell you that they are ten times as happy."
learning / knowledge / wisdom	"If you have an apple and I have an apple and we exchange these apples then you and I will still each have one apple. But if you have an idea and I have an idea and we exchange these ideas, then each of us will have two ideas."
life	"I want to be all used up when I die."
life	"Life is no brief candle to me. It is a sort of splendid torch, which I have got a hold of for the moment; and I want to make it burn as brightly as possible before handing it on to future generations."
life	"Life isn't about finding yourself. Life is about creating yourself."

Quotations by Henry David Thoreau (1817 - 1862), American writer, poet and philosopher:

| action / goals / initiative | "If you have built castles in the air, your work need not be lost. There is where they should be. Now put foundations under them." |

| attitude | "Be true to your work, your word and your friend." |

| attitude | "Do not lose hold of your dreams or aspirations. For if you do, you may still exist but you have ceased to live." |

| attitude | "I live in the present. I only remember the past, and anticipate the future." |

| friends / enemies | "Friends . . . they cherish one another's hopes. They are kind to one another's dreams." |

| life | "Many men go fishing all of their lives without knowing that it is not fish they are after." |

| life | "None are so old as those who have outlived enthusiasm." |

life	"The cost of a thing is the amount of what I will call life which is required to be exchanged for it, immediately or in the long run."
life	"The true harvest of my life is intangible - a little star dust caught, a portion of the rainbow I have clutched."
life	"When it's time to die, let us not discover that we have never lived."
success / failure	"If one advances confidently in the direction of one's dreams, and endeavors to live the life which one has imagined, one will meet with a success unexpected in common hours."
success / failure	"Success usually comes to those who are too busy to be looking for it."
success / failure	"We must walk consciously only part way toward our goal, and then leap in the dark to our success."

Quotations by Mark Twain, the pen name of Samuel Langhorne Clemens (1835 – 1910), American writer and humorist:

action / goals / initiative

"The secret of getting ahead is getting started. The secret of getting started is breaking your complex overwhelming tasks into small manageable tasks, and then starting on the first one."

attitude

"Always do right. This will gratify some people and astonish the rest."

attitude

"Common sense is a most uncommon virtue."

attitude

"Courage is resistance to fear, mastery of fear - not absence of fear."

attitude

"It's not the size of the dog in the fight, it's the size of the fight in the dog."

attitude

"Keep away from people who try to belittle your ambitions. Small people always do that, but the really great make you feel that you, too, can become great."

attitude

"Sing like nobody's listening, dance like nobody's watching, love like you've never been hurt, and live like it's heaven on earth."

change	"If you always do what you always did, you'll always get what you always got."
character	"If you tell the truth you don't have to remember anything."
children / family / parenting	"It is a wise child that knows its own father, and an unusual one that unreservedly approves of him."
friends / enemies	"If you are looking for friends when you need them, it's too late."
government / politics	"If you don't read the newspaper you are uninformed, if you do read the newspaper you are misinformed."
government / politics	"No man's life, liberty, or property is safe while the legislature is in session."
government / politics	"Suppose you were an idiot and suppose you were a member of Congress. But I repeat myself."
government / politics	"The only difference between a tax man and a taxidermist is that the taxidermist leaves the skin."

government / politics	"There is no distinctly native American criminal class...save Congress."
happiness	"The best way to cheer yourself up is to try to cheer somebody else up."
humor	"It usually takes more than three weeks to prepare a good impromptu speech."
humor	"In Paris they simply stared when I spoke to them in French; I never did success in making those idiots understand their own language."
leadership	"The right word may be effective, but no word was ever as effective as a rightly timed pause."
learning / knowledge / wisdom	"A classic is something that everybody wants to have read and nobody has.
learning / knowledge / wisdom	"A man who does not read good books does not have any advantage over the person who cannot read them."
life	"Don't go around saying the world owes you a living. The world owes you nothing. It was here first."

life	"Life would be infinitely happier if we could only be born at the age of eighty and gradually approach eighteen."
life	"Twenty years from now you will be more disappointed by the things you didn't do than by the ones you did do. So throw off the bowlines. Sail away from the safe harbor. Catch the trade winds in your sails. Explore. Dream. Discover."
optimism / pessimism	"The man who is a pessimist before forty-eight knows too much; if he is an optimist after it he knows too little."
success / failure	"Why not go out on a limb? That's where the fruit is."

Quotations by Johann Wolfgang von Goethe (1749 - 1832), German writer, philosopher and scientist:

action / goals / initiative   **"What you do, or dream you can, begin it. Boldness has genius, power and magic in it. Begin it now."**

attitude   **"There is nothing worse than aggressive stupidity."**

change   **"We must always change, renew, rejuvenate ourselves; otherwise we harden."**

character   **"Character develops itself in the stream of life."**

character   **"Nothing shows a man's character more than what he laughs at."**

learning/ knowledge / wisdom   **"In the end we retain from our studies only that which we practically apply."**

learning / knowledge / wisdom   **"Knowing is not enough; we must apply. Willing is not enough; we must do."**

learning / knowledge / wisdom	**"Nothing is more terrible than ignorance in action."**
learning / knowledge / wisdom	**"To accept good advice is but to increase one's own ability."**
life	**"Progress has not followed a straight ascending line, but a spiral with rhythms of progress and retrogression, of evolution and dissolution."**
life	**"Things which matter most must never be at the mercy of the things that matter least."**
time	**"We always have time enough, if we but use it right."**

Quotations by Denis Waitley (1933 -), American motivational speaker and writer, consultant and best-selling author:

action / goals / initiative	**"Change the changeable, accept the unchangeable, and remove yourself from the unacceptable."**
action / goals / initiative	**"Don't be a time manager, be a priority manager. Cut your major goals into bite-sized pieces. Each small priority or requirement on the way to ultimate goal becomes a mini goal in itself."**
attitude	**"Determination gives you the resolve to keep going in spite of the roadblocks that lay before you."**
attitude	**"Don't dwell on the past ... learn from it."**
attitude	**"Expect the best, plan for the worst, and prepare to be surprised."**
attitude	**"Goals provide the energy source that powers our lives. One of the best ways we can get the most from the energy we have is to focus it. That is what goals can do for us; concentrate our energy."**

attitude	"If you believe you can, you probably can. If you believe you won't, you most assuredly won't. Belief is the ignition switch that gets you off the launching pad."
attitude	"Losers live in the past. Winners learn from the past and enjoy working in the present toward the future."
attitude	"Losers make promises they often break. Winners make commitments they always keep."
attitude	"Our limitations and success will be based, most often, on your own expectations for ourselves. What the mind dwells upon, the body acts upon."
attitude	"Relentless, repetitive self talk is what changes our self-image."
attitude	"The winner's edge is not in a gifted birth, a high IQ, or in talent. The winner's edge is all in the attitude, not aptitude. Attitude is the criterion for success."
attitude	"Winners have the ability to step back from the canvas of their lives like an artist gaining perspective. They make their lives a work of art / an individual masterpiece."

attitude	"Winners take time to relish their work, knowing that scaling the mountain is what makes the view from the top so exhilarating."
children / family / parenting	"The greatest gifts you can give your children are the roots of responsibility and the wings of independence."
learning / knowledge / wisdom	"All of the top achievers I know are life-long learners... Looking for new skills, insights, and ideas. If they're not learning, they're not growing... not moving toward excellence."
success / failure	"Success is almost totally dependent upon drive and persistence. The extra energy required to make another effort or try another approach is the secret of winning."
time	"Time is the most precious element of human existence. The successful person knows how to put energy into time and how to draw success from time."

Quotations by John Wooden (1910 - 2010), American Hall of Fame basketball coach for UCLA who won a record 10 NCAA men's championships:

action / goals / initiative   **"For an athlete to function properly, he must be intent. There has to be a definite purpose and goal if you are to progress. If you are not intent about what you are doing, you aren't able to resist the temptation to do something else that might be more fun at the moment."**

action / goals / initiative   **"If you fail to prepare, you prepare to fail."**

attitude   **"A player who makes a team great is much more valuable than a great player."**

attitude   **"Don't let what you cannot do interfere with what you can do."**

attitude   **"If you don't have time to do it right, when will you have time to do it over?"**

attitude   **"It's not how big you are, it's how big you play."**

attitude   **"It's the little details that are vital. Little things make big things happen."**

attitude	"Talent is God given. Be humble. Fame is man-given. Be grateful. Conceit is self-given. Be careful."
attitude	"Why do we fear adversity, when we know that overcoming it is the only way to become stronger, smarter, and better?"
attitude	"You can't let praise or criticism get to you. It's a weakness to get caught up in either one."
attitude	"You can't live a perfect day without doing something for someone who will never be able to repay you."
character	"Be more concerned with your character than your reputation, because your character is what you really are, while your reputation is merely what others think you are."
life	"Things turn out best for the people that make the best of the way things turn out."
success / failure	"Success is peace of mind which is a direct result of self-satisfaction in knowing you did your best to become the best you are capable of becoming."

Quotations by Zig Ziglar (1926 -), American author, salesman, and motivational speaker.

action / goals / initiative	"If you want to reach a goal, you must 'see the reaching' in your own mind before you actually arrive at your goal."
attitude	"The main thing is to keep the main thing the main thing."
attitude	"You are the only person on earth who can use your ability."
attitude	"Your attitude, not your aptitude, will determine your altitude."
character	"The foundation stones for a balanced success are honesty, character, integrity, faith, love and loyalty."
character	"You will make a lousy anybody else, but you are the best you in existence."
life	"Life is too short to spend your precious time trying to convince a person who wants to live in gloom and doom otherwise. Give lifting that person your best shot, but don't hang around long enough for his or her bad attitude to pull you down. Instead, surround yourself with optimistic people."

life	"You must become a meaningful specific rather than a wandering generality."
success / failure	"Remember that failure is an event - not a person."
success / failure	"Success is the maximum utilization of the ability that you have."
success / failure	"You can have everything in life you want, if you will just help other people get what they want."

These are the compiler's Top 20 favorite quotations. This started out as a Top 10 list, but it was just too difficult to narrow 1,400 great quotations down to just 10!

Action / Goals / Initiative

"It had long since come to my attention that people of accomplishment rarely sat back and let things happen to them. They went out and happened to things."

Leonardo da Vinci (1452 - 1519), Italian architect, engineer, painter, sculptor, inventor and scientist.

Attitude

"Ability will never catch up with the demand for it."

Malcolm S. Forbes (1919 - 1919), American publisher of *Forbes* magazine.

"Excellence is the result of caring more than others think is wise, risking more than others think is safe, dreaming more than others think is practical, and expecting more than others think is possible."

Unknown

"He who laughs, lasts."

Robert Fulghum (1937 -), American author, painter, sculptor and former minister.

"Your attitude, not your aptitude, will determine your altitude."

Zig Ziglar (1926 -), American author, salesman, and motivational speaker.

Humor

"While not exactly disgruntled, she was far from being gruntled."

Unknown

Leadership

"Leadership is about capturing the imagination and enthusiasm of your people with clearly defined goals that cut through the fog like a beacon in the night."

Unknown

Life

"And in the end, it's not the years in your life that count. It's the life in your years."

Abraham Lincoln (1809 - 1865), 16th US President. His term of office was from 1861 to 1865 and included the American Civil War.

"Don't take life too seriously, you'll never get out of it alive."

Elbert Hubbard (1856 - 1915), American writer and editor.

"Life is not measured by the number of breaths we take, but the number of moments that take our breath away."

Maya Angelou (1928 -), American author and poet.

"Live with intention. Walk to the edge. Listen hard. Practice wellness. Play with abandon. Laugh. Choose with no regret. Appreciate your friends. Continue to learn. Do what you love. Live as if this is all there is."

Mary Anne Radmacher

"The best things in life aren't things."
Art Buchwald (1925 - 2007), American humorist best known for his long-running column in *The Washington Post.*

"There is no future in spending the present worrying about the past."

Unknown

"To love is to risk not being loved in return. To hope is to risk pain. To try is to risk failure, but risk must be taken because the greatest hazard in life is to risk nothing."

Unknown

"Twenty years from now you will be more disappointed by the things you didn't do than by the ones you did do. So throw off the bowlines. Sail away from the safe harbor. Catch the trade winds in your sails. Explore. Dream. Discover."

Mark Twain, the pen name of Samuel Langhorne Clemens (1835 - 1910), American writer and humorist.

Love / Relationships

"Perhaps they are not stars, but rather openings in heaven where the love of our lost ones pours through and shines down upon us to let us know they are happy."

Eskimo proverb.

Success / Failure

"Six essential qualities that are the key to success: sincerity, personal integrity, humility, courtesy, wisdom, charity."

Dr. William Menninger (1899 - 1966), American Co-Founder (with his brother Karl and his father) of The Menninger Foundation in Topeka, Kansas, an internationally known center for treatment of behavioral disorders.

"The greatest danger for most of us is not that our aim is too high and we miss it, but that it is too low and we reach it."

Michelangelo (1475 - 1564), Italian sculptor, painter, poet and architect of the Renaissance.

Time

"Our time is limited, so don't waste it living someone else's life. Don't be trapped by dogma — which is living with the results of other people's thinking. Don't let the noise of others' opinions drown out your own inner voice. And most important, have the courage to follow your heart and intuition. They somehow already know what you truly want to become. Everything else is secondary."

Steve Jobs (1955 -), American businessman and Co-Founder at Apple Inc., the inventor of Mac computers, iPods, iPhones and iPads.

"To achieve great things, two things are needed; a plan, and not quite enough time."

Leonard Bernstein (1918 - 1990), American conductor, composer and pianist.

Buchanan, Edna (1939 -), Americ	"Friends are the family we ch	84
	"True friends are those who r	179
Buchwald, Art (1925 - 2007), Am	"The best things in life aren'	163, 247
Buddha, Gautama a spiritual tea	"Holding onto anger is like gr	24
	"The secret of health for both	48
Buddhist saying.	"If you want to know your pas	4
Budgell, Eustace (1686 - 1737), E	"Friendship is a strong and ha	84
Buechner, Carl W.	"They may forget what you sa	126
Bueller, Ferris (played by Matthe	"Life moves pretty fast. If yo	156
Buffet, Jimmy (1946 -), American	"If we couldn't laugh, we wou	28
Buffett, Warren (1930 –), Ameri	"It takes 20 years to build a	33
Bull, Sitting (1831 - 1890), Hunk	"Let us put our minds togethe	79
Bullock, Sandra (1964 -), Americ	"Beginnings are usually scary	143
Burke, Edmund (1729 - 1797), Iri	"Nobody made a greater mist	159
	"The only thing necessary for	124
Burns, George (1896 - 1996), Am	"It's hard for me to get used	107
	"Too bad the only people who	109
Burroughs, John (1837 - 1921), a	"A man can fail many times, b	187
Buscaglia, Leo (1924 - 1998), Am	"The easiest thing to be in th	66
	"The most important thing in l	165
Bush, George H.W. (1924 -), 41st	"I have opinions of my own --	26
Bush, George W. (1946 -), Ameri	"They want the federal gover	93
Butler, Samuel	"Friendship is like money, eas	84
Byrne, Robert (1930 -), American	"Democracy is being allowed	88
Cabell, James Branch (1879 - 195	"The optimist proclaims that	185
Camara, Dom Helder (1909 - 199	"When we are dreaming alon	55
Cameron, Simon (1799 - 1889),	"An honest politician is one w	87
Campbell, Joseph (1904 - 1987),	"To find your own way is to fo	99
Cantor, Eddie (1892 - 1964), Am	"Slow down and enjoy life. It	162
Carey, Drew (1958 -), American c	"Oh, you hate your job? Why	107
Carey, Sandra	"Never mistake knowledge fo	137
Carlin, George (1937 - 2008), Am	"Don't sweat the petty things	103
Carlyle, Thomas (1795 - 1881), S	"I have a great ambition to di	149
Carnegie, Andrew (1835-1919), S	"As I grow older, I pay less a	14
	"People who are unable to m	40
Carnegie, Dale (1888 - 1955), Am	"Any fool can criticize, conde	69
	"Don't be afraid to give your	2
	"Instead of worrying about w	31
	"It isn't what you have, or wh	97
	"One person with a belief is w	39
	"The person who gets the far	197
Carter Jr., Hodding (1907 - 1972)	"There are two lasting beques	81

Earhart, Amelia (1897 - 1937), A	"The most difficult thing is t	165
Edelman, Marian Wright (1939 -)	"Be a good ancestor. Stand fo	143
	"Be real. Try to do what you s	15
	"Don't wait for, expect, or re	19
Edison, Thomas (1847 - 1931), A	"Genius is 1% inspiration and	22
	"Many of life's failures are p	191
	"Opportunity is missed by mo	192
	"Vision without execution is h	127
	"We haven't failed. We know	127
	"We shall have no better con	171
Edwards, Tryon (1809 - 1894), A	"Thoughts lead on to purpose	75
Ehrmann, Max (1872 – 1945), A	"With all its sham, drudgery,	173
Einstein, Albert (1879 - 1955), G	"Be profound, be funny, or be	15, 211
	"Common sense is the collecti	16, 211
	"Great spirits have always enc	23, 211
	"I never teach my pupils; I on	134, 212
	"If you can't explain it simpl	134, 212
	"Imagination is everything. It	151, 213
	"Imagination is more importa	135, 212
	"Insanity is doing the same th	31, 211
	"It is a miracle curiosity sur	32, 211
	"It is the supreme art of the	136, 212
	"Learn from yesterday, live fo	153, 213
	"Logic will get you from A to	157, 213
	"Most people say that is it is	73, 212
	"Strive not to be a success, b	193, 213
	"The difference between stup	138, 212
	"The level of thinking that go	139, 212
	"The Three Rules of Work: 1.	49, 211
	"There are two ways to live y	168, 213
	"Try not to become a man of s	75, 212
	"Two things are infinite: the	170, 213
	"Unthinking respect for autho	52, 211
	"We can't solve problems by	140, 213
Eisenhower, Dwight D. Army Ge	"An intellectual is a man who	132
	"I like to believe that people	89
	"Leadership is the art of gett	119
	"Pessimism never won any ba	184
	"You don't lead by hitting peo	130
Eliot, George (1819 - 1880), pen	"It's never too late to be who	33
	"No great deed is done by falt	37
Elliott, Walter (1842 - 1928), Am	"Perseverance is not a long ra	41

"Change is the law of life. And those who look only to the past or	63
"Change the changeable, accept the unchangeable, and remove y	1, 237
"Change what you cannot accept and accept what you cannot cha	64
"Character cannot be developed in ease and in quiet. Only throug	70
"Character develops itself in the stream of life."	70, 235
"Character is a journey, not a destination."	70
"Character is like a tree and reputation like a shadow. The shadow	70
"Character is like the foundation of a house - it is below the sur	71
"Character is long-standing habit."	71
"Character is made by what you stand for; reputation, by what yo	71
"Character is so largely affected by association, that we cannot a	71
"Character is the firm foundation stone upon which one must buil	71
"Character is the result of two things: mental attitude and the wa	71
"Character is what you are. Reputation is what people think you a	71
"Character is what you know you are, not what others think you	71
"Character, in the long run, is the decisive factor in the life of	72, 225
"Children are the world's most valuable resource and its best hop	26
"Children need love the most when they deserve it the least."	78
"Children need your presence much more than your presents."	78
"Children seldom misquote you. In fact, they usually repeat word	78
"Children spell love... T-I-M-E."	201
"Children will not remember you for the material things you provi	78
"Choose a job you like and you will never have to work a day of yo	113
"Coming together is a beginning, staying together is progress, and	113
"Common sense is a most uncommon virtue."	16, 231
"Common sense is not so common "	16
"Common sense is the collection of prejudices acquired by age eig	16, 211
"Consider how hard it is to change yourself; and you will understa	64
"Continuous effort - not strength or intelligence - is the key to	2, 207
"Courage doesn't always roar. Sometimes courage is the small v	16
"Courage is being afraid but going on anyhow."	16
"Courage is fear holding on a minute longer."	17
"Courage is not the absence of fear, but rather the judgment that	17
"Courage is resistance to fear, mastery of fear - not absence of f	17, 231
"Courage is what it takes to stand up and speak. Courage is also w	17, 237
"Criticism should always leave people with the feeling that they h	17
"Cynicism is an unpleasant way of saying the truth."	17
"Dance as though no one is watching. Love as though you've neve	144
"Death is more universal than life; everyone dies but not everyon	144
"Democracy is being allowed to vote for the candidate you dislike	88
"Democracy must be something more than two wolves and a she	88
"Desire is the key to motivation, but it's the determination and c	188

Here's some space to add your own favorite quotations:

_____

_____

_____

_____

_____

_____

_____

_____

_____

_____

_____

_____

_____

_____

_____

_____

_____

_____

_____

www.ingramcontent.com/pod-product-compliance
Lightning Source LLC
Chambersburg PA
CBHW020358100426
42812CB00001B/104